PRAISE FOR HONORING THE COVENANT

"Everyone is busy—married couples, especially with children, are extremely so. Yet to have a thriving marriage, couples must resist the temptation to make spiritual growth an afterthought. To aid busy couples, Fr. Magat offers a short reflection and meditation for each of the daily gospel readings throughout the year. This simple aid will be of great assistance to any couple wishing to deepen their interior life and strengthen their marriage."

—Most Rev. Salvatore J. Cordileone,
Archbishop of San Francisco

"*Honoring the Covenant* is a unique contribution to married life. Fr. Magat, in his straightforward and thought-provoking manner, challenges couples to deepen their faith together, instead of on separate tracks. This book will be a source of deep grace for both newlyweds and seasoned couples."

—Carrie Gress, PhD, author of *The End of Woman*,
Theology of Home, and *The Anti-Mary Exposed*

"If you and your spouse want to grow deeper in your relationship with the Lord and with each other, *Honoring the Covenant* by Fr. Jerome Magat is the perfect book for you. Fr. Magat has tapped his years of experience ministering to married couples to create a *lectio divina* that makes it easy for you and your spouse to unlock the mystery of couple prayer. His thoughtful mediations and provocative questions provide the perfect tool to help you uncover those areas in your marriage most in need of holy transformation and to celebrate those areas where you are living fully the gifts that God has given you through the Sacrament of Marriage. This is a must-read for any who wish to build up their marriage, their family, and the Church."

—Thérèse Bermpöhl, Executive Director,
Office of Family Life,
Catholic Diocese of Arlington, VA

"Jesus said, 'Where two or three are gathered together in my name, there am I in the midst of them' (Mt 18:20). The end of the day is the perfect time to use this book. *Honoring the Covenant* fills the gap so that couples can transform the last part of their day into a sacred, healing, grace-filled time. This book is a must-pray!"

—Fr. Keith O'Hare, Pastor,
St. Louis Catholic Church, Alexandria, VA

HONORING THE COVENANT

SUNDAY, SOLEMNITY, AND FEAST DAY MASS GOSPEL MEDITATIONS FOR BUSY MARRIED COUPLES

REV. JEROME A. MAGAT, STHD

ISBN 979-8-218-60151-5

Kindle Direct Publishing
Seattle, Washington
Printed in the United States of America

Front cover art: *Hochzeit zu Kana* (*The Wedding Feast at Cana*) by Julius Schnorr von Carolsfeld (1819), in the public domain: https://commons.wikimedia.org/wiki/File:Julius_Schnorr_von_Carolsfeld_-_The_Wedding_Feast_at_Cana_-_WGA21013.jpg

Front cover design by Margaret Mary Delehanty

Interior formatting by TeaBerryCreative.com

DEDICATION

This book is dedicated to Our Lady of Perpetual Help—the Daughter of the Father, Mother of the Son, and Spouse of the Holy Spirit. She is the fairest daughter of our race. She is our life, our sweetness, and our hope—the New Eve and our mother in the order of grace.

CONTENTS

FOREWORD

Amidst busy lives, we can easily postpone spiritual growth. Fr. Jerome Magat's *Honoring the Covenant* gives married couples an easy and concrete way to pause, reflect, and redirect their lives more fully to the things that really matter.

The short meditations provide an easy way to stay in touch with the Church's liturgy. The question(s) / prayer section that follows each short meditation helps enflesh the day's insight, applying it to the couple's life.

While intended for married couples, the meditations and questions can easily be adapted to one's own state in life.

Fr. Magat's simple and direct method, springing out of years of pastoral care for couples, helps take the guesswork out of "where to begin" praying. It facilitates conversation with God, which is the life of any Christian marriage.

—Most Reverend Michael F. Burbidge,
Bishop of Arlington

PREFACE

In the early 2000s, I served as a chaplain for a group of five married couples involved in TEAMS of Our Lady, a Marian marriage movement in the Catholic Church. I quickly observed a fact obvious to every married couple today: COUPLES ARE INCREDIBLY BUSY. In fact, they get so busy that there's always the temptation to make their spiritual growth an afterthought or a future project once retirement sets in. The couples for whom I have had the privilege of serving as chaplain know that growth in the interior life is a necessity for them and for every married couple NOW. These couples also know that marriage is a covenant and that it takes hard work to make it flourish. The marriage covenant and its growth in the lives of these couples is a priority and the animating force behind their day-to-day living. These couples have grown to see that is in the context of covenants that God has always dealt with his people and that this nuptial reality between God and the Church is the basis for the design of marriage between man and woman. That is why St. Paul, in Ephesians 5, explains how marriage between man and woman is a sign of Christ's love for his Church. "It is a great mystery," marvels St. Paul (Eph 5:32).

Given this backdrop, I have composed a series of meditations for the Sunday, Solemnity, and Feast Day Mass gospel readings throughout the liturgical year. *Honoring the Covenant* contains meditations that are simple, direct, and practical. They are designed for couples who want to make time to pray and are seeking brief and meaningful insights into the gospel reading of the day *vis à vis* their married life.

The format of the book is simple: Every entry includes the scriptural citation for the Mass gospel passage. Each meditation attempts to draw out insights from the Gospel as they apply to married life and usually concludes with a question or resolution to challenge the couple to further spiritual growth. This book is not meant to be exhaustive of all that has been written on the gospel passages of the year—it is intended to assist married couples in their journey towards eternal life. *Of course, nothing can replace attendance at Mass and worthy reception of Holy Communion.*

May the Blessed Virgin Mary continue to bless you and your marriage, securing for you all of the graces that you need or desire to bring to fulfillment the good work that God has begun in you until the coming of the Lord Jesus in glory.

ACKNOWLEDGEMENTS

I want to acknowledge the assistance of all of the married couples I have known and worked with over the past two decades, who contributed to this book by their lives of faith and inspired me to write these meditations. I am grateful for the many benefactors who have supported me in this work. In particular, I acknowledge the support of Carmen Segovia and Carrie Gress, PhD, whose encouragement and financial assistance helped me advance the work that led to the publication of this volume. I am especially thankful for the dedication and incredible hard work of Kim Guercio and Diana Pascoe, who committed to bringing my work to press once again. I am very grateful for the editorial and publishing expertise of Elizabeth Kantor and Tara Mayberry, whose guidance proved invaluable. I am indebted to these women for their gracious assistance and invoke the Lord's manifold blessings upon them. Finally, I am indebted to the clerics and laypersons who have endorsed this latest volume. It has been an honor to collaborate with them over the years.

HOW TO USE THIS BOOK

Honoring the Covenant is meant to be used alongside Sacred Scripture. The gospel readings for each day correspond to the gospel passage reading from the *Lectionary* (sacred book containing the readings) at Holy Mass.

To locate the correct liturgical day, it is best to consult the website for the United States Conference of Catholic Bishops (www.usccb.org). This site indicates the current liturgical day and provides the readings for Holy Mass. The gospel citation on the website should match the citation found in this book. The translation in your copy of the Scriptures may be slightly different from the translation used in the *Lectionary*. Feel free to use either translation.

SUNDAYS, SOLEMNITIES, AND FEAST DAYS OF ADVENT AND CHRISTMAS

FIRST SUNDAY OF ADVENT—YEAR A

GOSPEL: MATTHEW 24:37-44

Meditation

Advent (which means "coming to" or "arriving") is a season of preparation and watchfulness, marked by the constant theme of vigilance and decisiveness, very much present in today's Gospel. There are a few different levels of preparedness that we ought to consider: There's the ultimate preparedness for the return of the Lord in glory to judge the living and the dead. There's the particular preparedness associated with our own life story and our personal preparation to meet the Lord at death. And there is the daily vigilance of prayer and the nourishment of friendship with God that is very hard to cultivate in our secularized culture so given to Christmas celebrations when we are still weeks away from the actual liturgical celebration. While the world is busy carousing, our sanctuaries are decked in purple (a color of penance), the *Gloria* is not said at Sunday Mass, and we increase the amount of time available for the Sacrament of Penance. Sounds like Lent, no?

And it happens seemingly every year: By the time we get to the third or fourth Sunday of Advent, we are *so exhausted* from everything we have been working on to try to get materially ready for Christmas that many of us are just ready for Christmas to be over. This is hardly the disposition the Lord desires from us during what should be a season of joy and expectation.

Question(s) / Prayer

What are concrete ways in which we will prepare personally and as a couple to welcome Jesus at Christmas? Will we succumb to the worldly pressure to celebrate Christmas prematurely during the Advent season, without proper spiritual preparation? Will we allow ourselves to get caught up in the exhaustion of the season, so typical of the age? Or will we carve out time to reflect upon the year that has passed and to set spiritual goals for the next?

FIRST SUNDAY OF ADVENT—YEAR B

GOSPEL: MARK 13:33-37

Meditation

The Gospel's call to vigilance regarding the return of the Lord at the end of time evokes the second coming of the Lord. The Advent season is a time when we typically commemorate his historical first coming as man over two thousand years ago. These two comings of Christ—the first at the original Christmas and his second coming to judge the living and the dead—remind us of a simple truth: In this life, we live in his mercy. In the next life, we will live in his justice. It is quite easy to become very comfortable "where we are" and to assume that we live in God's good graces. And while we can live with confidence and filial trust in the Lord's promise to those who are faithful to him, we always run the risk of not keeping watch and of lacking the alertness necessary to be prepared to meet the Lord when he calls us home at a time we do not know.

Question(s) / Prayer

Are we vigilant in anticipating the return of the Lord, so that we make our ongoing growth in holiness a real priority? Are we content "where we are" without any sense of urgency to become more committed disciples of the Lord through the demands of our vocation? Do we presume our salvation based on a set of criteria that have little to no correspondence with what the Lord actually expects of us? Advent is a time of new beginnings. May we commit to humbling ourselves before the Lord of all history, who invites us to love him on his terms.

FIRST SUNDAY OF ADVENT—YEAR C
GOSPEL: LUKE 21:25-28, 34-36

Meditation

The secularization of Christmas and contemporary society's overemphasis on the material aspects of what began as a religious celebration challenge Catholics and other Christians to utilize the season of Advent for its true purpose: preparation for Christmas. The secularized version of Christmas begins on the Friday after Thanksgiving and ends on the evening of December 25. This presents a very difficult obstacle for Catholics who want to use Advent as a preparatory season for Christmas, since most Christmas office parties occur well before Christmas Day and the rush for gifts and the seasonal music heard on the airwaves can make Advent anything but preparatory.

The gospel passage for this First Sunday of Advent presents another contrast: Advent invites us to meditate upon the coming of the infant Jesus, nurtured in the womb of the Blessed Virgin Mary, and on the humility and poverty of his coming in the "fullness of time" (Gal 4:4). And yet the gospel passage presents the triumphal return of the Lord Jesus in all his glory, power, and might. In either scenario, the counsel imparted to us would be the same: "Beware that your hearts do not become drowsy from carousing and drunkenness and the anxieties of daily life, and that day catch you by surprise…" (Lk 21:34). In other words, whether we consider the return of Christ at the end of the world or meditate upon the events involving his first coming, preparedness ought to be our disposition.

Question(s) / Prayer

How often do we find ourselves overwhelmed by the material preparations for Christmas with no strength to prepare spiritually? We find ourselves "fitting prayer in" during Advent, instead of "fitting shopping in"—scheduling that less sublime activity around our prayer. While material and spiritual preparations need not be mutually exclusive, the latter should always take precedence over the former if we intend to use Advent well. Might we commit to setting aside time each night to pray the Joyful Mysteries of the Rosary? To reading the infancy narratives in Matthew and Luke? To making charitable donations to worthy causes that advance the Gospel?

SECOND SUNDAY OF ADVENT—YEAR A

GOSPEL: MATTHEW 3:1-12

Meditation

St. John the Baptist was a firebrand of a preacher, as demonstrated in today's Gospel. He must have been a compelling preacher to attract multitudes to the Judean desert to hear him. If you have ever been in a desert, the conditions are harsh and unforgiving. Most notably, John was even attracting Pharisees and Sadducees, members of the elite Jewish religious ruling class of Jerusalem and the region. And he did not mince his words, taking them to task for the sin of presuming their salvation. These elite rulers thought themselves to have no need of repentance because they were of the lineage of Abraham—the first of the Jewish patriarchs. And as long as they maintained their status and pedigree, they felt secure that their salvation was assured.

We ought to heed John's warning as well—it is not difficult to fall into the sin of presumption ourselves. We can delude ourselves into thinking that we are in a safe, comfortable place in life. We may have secure finances, professional and social prestige, and all the marks of worldly success. We may be very devout and pious Catholics. We can begin to presume that just because we have all the appearances of piety and devotion and/or worldly success, our salvation is secure and we have no need for repentance.

Question(s) / Prayer

Do I/we presume our salvation? Or like St. Paul, are we working out our salvation in "fear and trembling" (Phil 2:12)? Do we understand the science of the saints, who never thought of themselves as being holy, but discovered that the closer they drew near to Christ, the more they saw their character faults and sins? This realization never produced despondency or despair in the saints. Rather, it increased their resolve to be truly holy—to be given over to the Lord in all aspects of their lives and always aware of their complete dependence on his grace.

SECOND SUNDAY OF ADVENT—YEAR B

GOSPEL: MARK 1:1-8

Meditation

The first verse of Mark's Gospel is highly subversive. Mark had just witnessed St. Peter's brutal execution by crucifixion by Nero near the Vatican hill in Rome, and yet he declares *evangelion* (gospel or good news of military victory in Greek). He then goes on to declare that the victor is Jesus Christ, the Son of God. The title "Son of God" was reserved for the emperor. In effect, Mark is writing that the true emperor is not Caesar, but Jesus and that he is the true military victor, testified by the martyrdom of the Roman church, especially St. Peter. This is the interpretive lens for understanding St. John the Baptist's exhortation to make straight the way of the Lord.

Whenever a king or emperor would visit a town built on a hill, the typical switchback paths leading up to the town or city would be cleared away and a dirt ramp built to spare the dignitary from making a circuitous trip up to the town. This is the consummate Advent metaphor—to make Christ's way and his arrival to reign in the city of our soul direct, simple, and uncomplicated so that his *evangelion* of glad tidings of victory in us can become a reality.

Question(s) / Prayer

Do we make Jesus' path to our hearts circuitous, complicated, and compromised? Or are we disposed to make it direct, simple, and uncomplicated so that his *evangelion* of glad tidings of victory in us can become a reality? What parts of our marriage remain unconverted and not given to his supreme reign of peace and love? What do we hold back from the Prince of Peace? Are we prepared to begin anew and allow him to have dominion over our lives? Or do we insist on controlling all outcomes and processes as if we are the main protagonists of the story of our lives?

SECOND SUNDAY OF ADVENT—YEAR C

GOSPEL: LUKE 3:1-6

Meditation

Today's Gospel describes how St. John the Baptist "went throughout the whole region of the Jordan, proclaiming a baptism of repentance for the forgiveness of sins" (Lk 3:3). Repentance denotes a turning or a change of mind, as well as moral conversion. It is the central message of the preaching of both St. John the Baptist and the Lord himself. But repentance is often hard and uncomfortable. It suggests that we need to change and that there is a deficit of holiness in us. It is particularly difficult to grasp in an age that no longer recognizes sin. Repentance implies humility and while most persons desire to be humble in principle, the humiliating work of making a sincere examination of conscience and confessing one's sins in the Sacrament of Penance is something most would prefer to avoid. It is not uncommon for individuals to rationalize, "I don't need to go to confession. After all, I haven't killed anyone...." And yet, when couples go to confession frequently and with devotion, they find themselves becoming more patient with one another because as they get into the habit of asking for pardon, they find themselves more generous in showing mercy. This softening of hearts is so crucial to helping couples remain in love.

Question(s) / Prayer

Lord, grant us the humility to admit and confess our sins. May we be quick to forgive, quick to apologize, and quick to turn to you in confidence. May the mercy we experience in the Sacrament of Penance be the hallmark of the mercy we show one another in the contradictions and disagreements that are a part of any marriage. May your mercy soften our hearts to be kind and merciful like the Father.

THIRD SUNDAY OF ADVENT—YEAR A

GOSPEL: MATTHEW 11:2-11

Meditation

Today's Gospel highlights the importance of recognizing Jesus in our midst. Concretely, we encounter Jesus in the sacraments. In this way, not only do we have Jesus among us—he actually makes his home *within* us through the life of sanctifying grace given to us at Baptism and augmented and specified through the other sacraments. The universal call to holiness is specified through the two sacraments of vocation: Holy Matrimony and Holy Orders.

Moreover, we are reminded in the writings of St. Paul that there is a crucial connection between our lives of grace and our worthiness to receive Jesus in the Eucharist. For many, many Catholics, there is a great disconnect here—they ignore Paul's words to the Corinthians: that one must examine oneself for serious sin and if one partakes of the Lord's Body and Blood unworthily, one becomes guilty of the Body and Blood of the Lord.

In this month replete with consumerism, the pattern of picking and choosing gifts transfers itself to how we connect our life to Christ with our reception of him in the Eucharist—as if the Eucharist were just another consumer product to be had. When we don't recognize the connection between the state of our soul and receiving Jesus, we do worse than the Jewish leaders who did not recognize the historical Jesus in their midst.

Question(s) / Prayer

Lord, help us to identify the disconnects in our sacramental practice—to remember that in order to benefit from the sacraments (especially the Eucharist), we need to be properly disposed to receive their attendant graces. May we understand deeply that the sacraments are not merely rituals or ceremonies. Rather, they are encounters with the Trinity that are intended to animate the life of sanctifying grace we received in Baptism. May we have eyes to see and hearts to understand that the Sacrament of Holy Matrimony offers special graces that will help us to live out our baptismal dignity within a particular state of life and that recognizing the movements of grace is in fact the ordinary way in which we can recognize Jesus trying to live within us.

THIRD SUNDAY OF ADVENT—YEAR B

GOSPEL: JOHN 1:6-8,19-28

Meditation

St. John the Baptist gives courageous and clear witness to the Lord. He speaks of Jesus with boldness and authority. It is clear that John's entire life is oriented towards preparing the way for Jesus to fulfill his mission. Famously, John the Baptist challenges his hearers to "make straight the way of the Lord" (Jn 1:23). As we have seen, this would have evoked an ancient practice of redirecting switchback trails leading to the top of a town so as to prevent a visiting dignitary from having to take a circuitous route to the town or city above. A more direct path was carved out and shaped so as to make the dignitary's visitation easier and more elegant. In other words, John the Baptist is calling his hearers to simplify their response to the Lord. The response of an authentic disciple should be uncompromised and uncomplicated. It should be direct and non-circuitous. This is the most authentic way to give witness to Christ, and it takes the type of clarity and courage that John the Baptists lived as the Lord's precursor.

Question(s) / Prayer

Do we realize that the longest distance we will travel in life is the eighteen inches between our heads and hearts? Are we prepared to carve out straight paths in the manner in which we live and the simplicity with which our married love is demonstrated daily? Do we overcomplicate and compromise on those things which ought to be straightforward and sincere? Or do we communicate in ways that engender honesty and transparency?

THIRD SUNDAY OF ADVENT—YEAR C

GOSPEL: LUKE 3:10-18

Meditation

Commensurate with the repentance John the Baptist preached was a deep sense of justice and fairness that his hearers were called to practice. Luke cites several specific exhortations John the Baptist gives to soldiers, sinners (tax collectors), and ordinary persons. This should provoke a response in the lives of the married—to treat one's spouse with fairness and justice and to be sensitive to one's obligations to one's spouse. But obligation is the least one ought to do—true love always seeks the best thing one can do for the other. Moving from mere obligation (justice) to love is a sign of spiritual and marital maturity. It is one of the hallmarks of marital health and bliss and a sign of connectedness.

Question(s) / Prayer

Lord, help us to give without counting the cost. Help us to transcend mere justice and reach a place of mature love that seeks to make the path to you easier and lighter for the other. May we find ourselves dissatisfied with seeking the least we can do for our spouse. Rather, let us discover the grace to be motivated to do our best for them, according to your sweet yoke of freedom and virtue. In this way, may our spouse know that they are loved and cherished by the other—the antidote to feeling being taken for granted.

FOURTH SUNDAY OF ADVENT—YEAR A

GOSPEL: MATTHEW 1:18-24

Meditation

The word "betrothed," used to describe the relationship between St. Joseph and our Lady, is often (and incorrectly) understood as "engaged." However, St. Joseph and the Blessed Virgin Mary were already married, not engaged, when she conceived Jesus by the power of the Holy Spirit. At a betrothal, the husband and wife exchanged marital consent, and then the husband went away for a year to prepare a home for his new bride (and the ensuing family). Meanwhile, the wife would go back and live with her parents until the day when the husband took her into his home. Notice how Matthew refers to Joseph as the husband of Mary and the angel assures Joseph not to be afraid to take Mary "your wife into your home" (Mt 1:20). In sum, today's passage contains at least three references to Joseph and Mary as husband and wife. Why do so many erroneously conflate betrothal and engagement? Probably by a projection of Western cultural dating and marriage customs onto a Semitic culture. Today's Gospel not only relates the story of the conception of the Lord but also challenges us to accept the story in its own context, without projecting our own biases.

Question(s) / Prayer

Do I accept the mysteries of the faith as related in the Scripture on its own terms, or do I unconsciously project my own limited understanding on the Word of God? Similarly, do I project my own biases onto the thought patterns and behaviors of my spouse, perhaps unconsciously expecting them to act and think exactly like me? Or am I prepared to accept my spouse for who they are and to respect the life experiences they bring to our marriage, which can enrichen my understanding within the confines of Christian morality and conduct?

FOURTH SUNDAY OF ADVENT—YEAR B

GOSPEL: LUKE 1:26-38

Meditation

At the time of the Annunciation (depicted in today's Gospel), Nazareth was an obscure village of fewer than thirty habitations. It was so unknown to many in Israel that nearly 75 percent of maps of the Holy Land at the time did not even mention its location. It is in this smallness and obscurity that God wrote the greatest story of his love for humanity, by sending his Son to an unknown maiden, to be nurtured and raised in relative anonymity. It is a remarkable reminder that God does not need the largess of human conventions to do his greatest work. Rather, what he "needs" is the faithful and humble cooperation of servants who echo our Lady's "*Fiat mihi secundum verbum tuum* (May it be done unto me according to your word)" (Lk 1:38). This is also true of the path to sanctity for most: It will almost always occur quietly in marriages and families, without any fanfare or spectacle. It happens when ordinary persons produce extraordinary fruits for the Kingdom by simply being properly disposed to grace. It happens when ordinary persons are willing to be led by the Spirit and to become less self-determined and self-made.

Question(s) / Prayer

Can we sense the Lord leading us in our marriage, or are we too entirely self-sufficient or self-determined or self-made? Is Christ the protagonist in our marriage, or are we the main protagonists who invoke Christ only when our resources run out or when we discern a need for wisdom and insight or moral direction? As Christ himself is the marriage between humanity and divinity (in his two natures), do we rely on him to sanctify and vivify our marriage? Are we too self-dependent, so that we seek to enrich our marriage with worldly wisdom versus supernatural wisdom? Are we content with living small, quiet, and humble lives that are obedient to the Father?

FOURTH SUNDAY OF ADVENT—YEAR C

GOSPEL: LUKE 1:39-45

Meditation

Echoing today's gospel passage, the Preface prayer for today's Mass states that "the Virgin Mother longed for him with love beyond all telling, John the Baptist sang of his coming and proclaimed his presence when he came. It is by his gift that we already rejoice at the mystery of his Nativity, so that he may find us watchful in prayer and exultant in his praise." The gospel passage challenges us to ask if we welcome our Lady and our Lord into our lives with joy, or do we see their presence as a limit on our freedom and the way of life we would like to pursue? John the Baptist's fetal recognition of the presence of the Lord challenges us to ask if we are attuned to the Lord's presence in our lives or if we find ourselves living as if God does not even exist. We can often become so distracted and enamored with the visible world that we can become inured to the invisible world of grace all around us.

Question(s) / Prayer

Father, help us to cultivate a more refined recognition of your immediate presence in our marriage and family. Like John the Baptist and Elizabeth, may we constantly rejoice in knowing that you are near. As it is so easy to become forgetful of you, inflame us with the grace of intentionality to seek and honor you in all aspects of our lives, not simply the dimensions of our lives where we find you convenient or agreeable to our preferences and tastes.

SOLEMNITY OF THE IMMACULATE CONCEPTION OF THE BLESSED VIRGIN MARY—DECEMBER 8

GOSPEL: LUKE 1:26-38

Meditation

The Church makes an audacious claim regarding the Immaculate Conception: In an anticipatory way, Mary enjoyed the merits of Jesus' redemptive sacrifice at Calvary so that at the moment of her conception, she was preserved from Original Sin in order to pass on perfect humanity to Jesus—the perfect victim and priest whose death opened the gates of heaven and reconciled us to the Father. Remarkably, today's Gospel portrays Jesus' conception, not Mary's. And why? Because the angel Gabriel in addressing Mary states (in Greek), "Hail Mary, you who have been full of grace" (Lk 1:28)—already alluding to her privileged status as the Immaculate Conception. This dramatic intervention in salvation history became the proximate means for the Incarnation (God become man in the person of Jesus Christ). It is worth noting that the disobedience of one married woman (Eve) was overturned by the *Fiat* of another married woman (Mary). God chose to intervene in a unique way through the person of the Blessed Virgin Mary, the humble, gentle maiden of Nazareth who was unknown to humanity at the moment of the Annunciation but is now the most renowned woman of all time.

Question(s) / Prayer

Lord, help us to place our marriage under the protective mantle of the Blessed Mother. May we always trust that she, who lived the married life, has a particular solicitude for us who live her vocation and who aspire for your will to become our greatest desire. May we dedicate ourselves daily to a complete openness to the promptings of your grace and imitate her perfect discipleship marked by a spirit of humility, gentleness, and total docility. May we echo her *Fiat* (Be it done to me as you say) and find ourselves being less self-determined and more open to being led by the Holy Spirit. O Mary, conceived without sin, pray for us who have recourse to thee!

FEAST OF OUR LADY OF GUADALUPE—DECEMBER 12

GOSPEL: LUKE 1:26-38

Meditation

Today's gospel narrative is the same passage used for the Immaculate Conception, but here we focus our attention upon the angel Gabriel's message to our Lady to not be afraid. These words were echoed by Our Lady of Guadalupe when she spoke to St. Juan Diego in Mexico in 1531—reassuring him not to be startled and ultimately to trust in her maternal intercession. We all carry many preoccupations and worries in this life, but if we are honest, so few of them regard what should be our top priority—concern for our salvation. We can be scared to broach this topic, let alone ponder its importance in the long view of our earthly sojourn. Like our Lady at Nazareth and like St. Juan Diego in Mexico, we are reminded that the Lord is really in charge. May we learn to trust this simple but hard-to-accept truth.

Question(s) / Prayer

Lord, help us to worry about those things that *really* matter. Help us to re-orient and re-focus our lives so that we have as much concern for our holiness as we do for so many of the trivial details of our earthly lives. Help us to cultivate deep and abiding trust in your plan for our lives. May the docility you expressed at Nazareth, imitated in the docility St. Juan Diego showed in Mexico, help us to discover an interior freedom that puts all of our earthly cares in their proper perspective.

SOLEMNITY OF THE NATIVITY OF THE LORD (CHRISTMAS)—MASS DURING THE NIGHT—DECEMBER 24

GOSPEL: LUKE 2:1-14

Meditation

We are well familiar with the struggle the Holy Family faced in Bethlehem to find a place for our Lady to give birth to the Lord "because there was no room for them in the inn" (Lk 2:7). One of the time-honored traditions in Hispanic cultures is the custom of celebrating *Las Posadas* (the inns, in Spanish) in which a boy and girl dress up as St. Joseph and the Blessed Virgin Mary and knock on several doors in a house or even a school (depending on where it is celebrated). Within each room is a group of persons who let the Holy Family know that there is no room for them in the inn. Finally, the couple knocks on a door wherein the occupants welcome them with joy, and a fiesta ensues. This is a metaphor for the inn of our soul. Jesus was born once in Bethlehem over two millennia ago, but it is up to each person to accept him with joy or reject him—on his terms, not merely our own. Christmas is an invitation to welcome Christ into the often crowded inn of our soul and to make plenty of room for him so that he can be born within us, mystically.

Question(s) / Prayer

Lord, help us to welcome you and our Lady and St. Joseph into the inns of our souls. May we never reject you, as so many innkeepers rejected you on Christmas night. And may we welcome you with joy, on your terms—always ready to make your presence among us our top priority and concern. May we never be too busy to make you our most welcomed guest! And when we accept you with joy, may we be willing to make those accommodations easy and uncomplicated. May every temptation to compromise be jettisoned from our souls so that all who know us as a couple married in Christ also know from our example that you are to be loved above all others.

SOLEMNITY OF THE NATIVITY OF THE LORD (CHRISTMAS)—MASS DURING THE DAY—DECEMBER 25

GOSPEL: JOHN 1:1-18

Meditation

Hearers of today's Gospel are often surprised that there is no mention of the Holy Family or the event of the Nativity or the shepherds or the Magi. Rather, St. John is writing in about the year AD 95, on the island of Patmos, Greece, reflecting on the profound transformation that he experienced thanks to the intense personal encounter he had with Christ. John does not recount the historical events surrounding the birth of Christ. Instead, he marvels at God the Father's profound mercy in sending us his Only-Begotten Son to save us from our sins. This should cause us to consider the reason for Christmas: the birth of Our Savior. But the notion of a Savior only makes sense if one recognizes the reality of sin, since it is from sin and eternal death that Christ saved us. In other words, if one does not recognize sin, one has no need of a Savior. And if one has no need for a Savior, Christmas is just another annual cultural ritual, with no personal significance. In such a paradigm, Christ can be kept at a distance, as if another accessory to the kingdom of the ego. There is hardly any room for the Prince of Peace to reign in such a place. Hence, the recognition of sin in one's life is one of the most liberating things one can experience since it tells the truth about who one is and makes Christmas not only joyful—but absolutely necessary!

Question(s) / Prayer

Father in heaven, may we express profound gratitude for the grand condescension you offer us in sending us Jesus to take on our humanity in all things but sin and to suffer and die so that we might have eternal life. May we readily confess our sins sacramentally, always cognizant of our need for our Savior. May our celebration of Christmas with this disposition help us to come face to face with the reality of sin in our lives and make us joyful that the Lord has indeed come to save us!

FEAST OF THE HOLY FAMILY OF JESUS, MARY, AND JOSEPH—SUNDAY WITHIN THE OCTAVE OF CHRISTMAS

GOSPEL: MATTHEW 2:13-15, 19-23 (YEAR A) / LUKE 2:22-40 (YEAR B) / LUKE 2:41-52 (YEAR C)

Meditation

Why did Jesus Christ, the all-powerful Son of God, need a family? Surely he could have taken care of himself without one. He took a family for the same reasons that he became man: so that he could be like us in all things except sin. As the saints of the early Church used to say, "He did not redeem what he did not take up." Jesus had a family as a sign of the reality that families too are saved, are meant to be instruments of salvation. The purpose of families in God's plan is to continue the natural line of generation and to get us to heaven. Every person in a family is meant to help the others to grow in goodness, holiness, and truth. That's the way that it's *meant* to be, anyway. But too many times, that's not the way that it actually *is*, because our sins and our selfishness get in the way.

How do families become holy? First each member of the family has to put the will of God before all else. The first concern of every family should be to do what God wants done in any given situation, and to avoid offending him by sin. Second, family members must have a commitment to grow in prayer and virtue. It's usually a lack of virtue (pride, selfishness, intemperance, bad temper, lack of self-control, jealousy of some family member, etc.) that causes the conflicts in a family. Moreover, it is not enough simply not to sin; God deserves our best effort, and in a family we also owe it to the others and even to ourselves to do well, to seek to be always more virtuous. It's hard to do that alone; that's another reason why a family can be such an aid to sanctity—we don't have to do it alone. Virtues are developed by witnessing them in the lives of others, imitating people who live them, and practicing the good habits over and over in our own lives until they become a part of us. Of course, by the same token, a family that does not seek holiness or virtue can be an anchor causing us to drown. If that is the case, then we must remember another key principle: acceptance of suffering. Patience and love can make any trial something that brings a family closer together. If we do not accept the trials of life together, then they will be a wedge that divides our families.

Question(s) / Prayer

Do we intentionally cultivate holiness in our marital relationship? Or do we seek to retain a little independence from God—a small bubble of selfishness? When trouble arises, is my first instinct to save myself rather than save the marriage? Do we look at our children as social accessories rather than persons? Do we push our kids to do all the "right" activities and apply to all the "right" schools more out of a concern for appearances than for their holiness? Do we cultivate a spirit of sacrifice and service? Do we recognize that, in the end, holiness in our families depends not on doing great things, but in constantly doing *all* things for God? Do we see that this leads to true love within the family? Do we accept the truth that true love within a family leads to holiness, and a life of holiness leads to heaven? May our family, by the grace of God, pursue a life of holiness oriented to heaven!

SOLEMNITY OF MARY, MOTHER OF GOD— JANUARY 1

GOSPEL: LUKE 2:16-21

Meditation

We have all observed the trusting way in which young children run to a loving mother and relish her embrace of tenderness and unadulterated love and delight. It is within this embrace that they feel safe and cherished. Today's solemnity invites us to approach our mother in the order of grace with the same confidence, knowing that we are loved and accepted. This is no superficial or calculated or passive love. Instead, it is the pure gaze of a mother who loves each of us as her children—interceding for us and communicating God's graces into the world according to our true needs. True spiritual children of the Blessed Virgin Mary turn to her with warmth, devotion, and joy. In her gaze, they sense their own vocation to personal holiness—to imitate such a lovable and venerable mother. Even those who have not experienced authentic maternal love from their natural mother can experience this closeness to our Lady. Recent saints such as St. Thérèse of Lisieux and Pope St. John Paul II have turned to our Lady upon the loss of their natural mothers and experienced her gentle embrace and protection. We begin a new year with our Lady, confident in her constant devotion to us, her children.

Question / Prayer

What is the status of our relationship with our mother, Mary? Do we turn to her with confidence, making constant recourse to her maternal protection and intercession? Would our marriage be described as Marian, in the sense that it is always focused on heeding her advice at Cana: "Do whatever he tells you" (Jn 2:5)? Do we cultivate the quiet, gentle, and contemplative spirit with which she nurtured the Holy Family in Nazareth? Is she our example for the life of the domestic church of the home? Might this new year find us turning to her through our devotion to the Rosary, offering each *Ave* as a rose in her crown of glory? We pray that our Lady will teach us to pray and to love, with the Lord always before us.

SOLEMNITY OF THE EPIPHANY OF THE LORD—THE SUNDAY BETWEEN JANUARY 2 AND JANUARY 8

GOSPEL: MATTHEW 2:1-12

Meditation

The events surrounding the Epiphany juxtapose the posture and the dispositions of the Magi and Herod. The Magi are men rooted in science who travel in faith to pay homage to the newborn King of the Jews. Naturally, they are drawn to where one might expect a newborn king to be—the local king's palace (hence their encounter with Herod). Metaphorically, the Magi represent men who have it all—immense wealth, intelligence, and time (most persons in this era lived a hand-to-mouth existence). But in spite of having every human comfort and advantage, they sense an incompleteness in their lives—the desire for an encounter with God. And so they set out from the East (their particular places of origin are not specified), combining faith and reason (astronomy) to find the Lord. Meanwhile, Herod reacts fearfully and recklessly. The Lord represents a threat to his kingdom, even though our Lord has no army, no followers, and none of the usual means of political or military aggression. Herod's fear, irrational as it is, corrupts his heart and compels him to launch the infamous massacre of the Holy Innocents.

There is in each of us the Magi and Herod. The Magi attitudes and dispositions rejoice in the Lord and seek him without reserve. The Herod attitude is fearful—handicapped by an attachment to comfort and the status quo, threatened by the invitation to conversion. It's the same attitude that fears having a larger family or making the Faith a genuine priority in the family. It's the fear that convinces us that we are in good place, even as that very attitude of complacency tempts us to spiritual mediocrity.

Question(s) / Prayer

Lord, help us to hear your voice above our own. May the peace your Kingdom brings help us to reject all fear and trepidation, especially when we sense a call to deeper conversion and spiritual progress. Grant us the grace to rejoice in you always and to use whatever means we have to seek you like the Magi. May we put aside all comfort and safety to embark on the spiritual journey to possess you and be possessed by you. Help us to recognize the Herod voices in our lives, which tempt us to reject you because we fear what a more committed discipleship may demand of us.

FEAST OF THE BAPTISM OF THE LORD—THE SUNDAY AFTER EPIPHANY, OR THE FOLLOWING MONDAY IF EPIPHANY IS CELEBRATED ON JANUARY 7 OR 8

(This feast is the First Sunday in Ordinary Time.)

GOSPEL: MATTHEW 3:13-17 (YEAR A) / MARK 1:7-11 (YEAR B) / LUKE 3:15-16, 21-22 (YEAR C)

Meditation

The ancient liturgical prayers for this feast marvel at how the lamp (signifying John the Baptist) is humbled by the request of the sun (signifying the Son) for baptism. The prayers compare John the Baptist to a voice and the Lord to the Word of God (*Logos*, in Greek) and speak of the servant (John the Baptist) baptizing the master (Jesus). The prayers marvel time and again at the Lord's humility—his willingness to condescend to a baptism he does not need in order to elevate and sanctify Baptism to the most fundamental sacrament in the Church's life. How immense the Lord's love for us shines through! Come, let us adore him!

A great saint of the last century said that the real crisis in the Church is not the sinfulness of its members or the lack of integrity of its leaders. Rather, the real crisis in the Church is a crisis of Baptism. If more Catholics lived up to their baptismal dignity, what a different world we would live in! If we took more seriously all that the Sacrament of Baptism demands of us and committed ourselves to living out our baptismal dignity, how much more holy marriage and family life could be …

Question(s) / Prayer

What obstacles do we put in the way of living out our baptismal dignity? Are we vigilant to guard ourselves and our family from influences that are not of the Lord? Are we steadfast to curb or eliminate the secular voices that surround us and are communicated through so much of popular media and music today? Do we even bother to consider if our forms of entertainment are appropriate for persons who have such an exalted baptismal dignity as we do? Do we prioritize frequent confession to renew and refresh our baptismal zeal? Do we understand what happened us at Baptism and its consequences for lives of faith and morals?

SUNDAYS OF LENT, THE TRIDUUM, AND SUNDAYS OF EASTER

FIRST SUNDAY OF LENT

GOSPEL: MATTHEW 4:1-11 (YEAR A) / MARK 1:12-15 (YEAR B) / LUKE 4:1-13 (YEAR C)

Meditation

The First Sunday of Lent is always dedicated to depictions of the forty-day temptation of Christ in the desert. While Mark's version is quite compact, Matthew and Luke expand upon the experience of the Lord and his spiritual combat with the Devil. Unlike all of us, who suffer from the wound of Original Sin, Jesus (and Mary) did not have to endure the burden of concupiscence (disordered desires) that causes the internal struggle we can all feel when temptations occur. The Lord (like our Lady) was only tempted from the outside, making the Devil's beguiling even more poignant. In Matthew's account, Jesus is tempted to sensuality in the first temptation (turning stones to bread)—a temptation of the flesh. In the second instance, the Lord is tempted to test divine providence (throwing himself from the pinnacle of the Temple). In the third temptation, Jesus is tempted to accept worldly power by worshipping the Devil himself. In Luke's account, the second and third temptation are in reverse order, beguiling the Lord to abandon his mission to save the world by his glorious Cross. In sum, Jesus is tempted to abandon his vocation to save us. Thankfully, the Lord overcomes the temptation, and the rest is HIStory.

Question(s) / Prayer

Lord, come to our assistance in avoiding the temptation to keep our eyes on the "greener grass" on the other side of the fence of our marital covenant, especially when our relationship hits a rough patch. May we recognize that in order to emerge victorious in our discipleship, we must persevere and endure many trials, imitating your constancy and grittiness. In a world so given to quick solutions and self-actualization by "discovering ourselves" may we find our true identity in you, who refused to abandon us. Instead, you preferred to suffer for us so that we might have everlasting life! We express our abiding gratitude for your sacrifice. Help us to accept the same in this life, knowing that our perseverance pleases you and resonates with your own experience of temptation.

SECOND SUNDAY OF LENT

GOSPEL: MATTHEW 17:1-9 (YEAR A) / MARK 9:2-10 (YEAR B) / LUKE 9:28B-36 (YEAR C)

Meditation

Recorded in all three synoptic Gospels (Matthew, Mark, Luke), the spectacle of the Transfiguration is often referred to as Christ's pledge of future glory. Just two weeks prior to Holy Week, this event would be seared into the memories of Peter, James, and John and steel them against the devastation of Good Friday. These three apostles experienced a foretaste of the glorified Christ, whom they would experience at length post-Resurrection. Peter's reaction is notable in all three accounts—he desires to build tents or booths or shrines to the Lord, Moses, and Elijah, almost as if to capture the magnificence of the experience. In other words, Peter wants to bask in the glory of the Transfiguration. However, Jesus has a mission to accomplish, and miles away from Mount Tabor (the mountain of the Transfiguration), Jesus will climb another mountain—Calvary, to suffer and die a most ignominious death. Jesus and the three Apostles, along with the other nine, will have to descend the glory of Mount Tabor and eventually traverse through the Kidron Valley into Gethsemane, before Christ suffers on Calvary on the way to the glory of Easter. This is the pattern for every disciple. To experience the glory of heaven, we need to traverse through this *lacrimarum valle* (vale of tears), as we recite in the Hail, Holy Queen (*Salve Regina*). Rather than try to bring heaven down to earth, the Transfiguration compels us to raise our sights up towards heaven and the glory that can be ours if we are faithful and persevering.

Question(s) / Prayer

Do we desire all the benefits of marriage, without the crosses that come along with it? Are we lacking in resilience to weather the storms that any marriage endures? Are we constantly striving for the "perfect" life, only to discover the emptiness that "having it all" brings us if we are not grounded in the Lord, who showed us the depths of his love in suffering? What are we willing to suffer for the sake of flourishing in our marriage? Are we just in survival mode because of deficits we fail to address meaningfully and consistently? Do we just prefer to stay up on the heights of the mountains without tackling the hard work that life in the valley demands of us?

THIRD SUNDAY OF LENT—YEAR A

GOSPEL: JOHN 4:5-42

Meditation

The remarkable and intricate conversation between Jesus and the Samaritan woman at the well has been the subject of much commentary over the millennia of Christian thought. But one line in particular stands out: Stunned by the Lord's ability to peer deeply into her life and her sordid past, the Samaritan woman tells her fellow townsmen, "He told me everything I have done" (Jn 4:39). Before the Lord, nothing about this woman is hidden. Nothing is unknown to him. And in spite of her sinful past, the Lord still thirsts for her soul, symbolized by water. The Lord is not a passive bystander when it comes to loving us. Rather, he is active and engaged and pursues each of us with intentionality. As lethargic and indifferent as we can become when it comes to loving him, the Lord maintains the opposite posture. This woman knows that Jesus is not just a prophet. Rather, he is Messiah and Lord. Her manner of addressing Jesus evolves throughout the length of the conversation to reflect this sure but certain realization.

Question(s) / Prayer

As much as we may strive to discover the Lord, are we as willing as the Samaritan woman at the well to be discovered *by* him? Are we willing to lay bare our weaknesses and deficits before him so that he can purify them and make us whole? Do we allow the Lord to pursue us, or are we indifferent to his desire for each of us, personally? Is our response frequent and heartfelt celebration of the Sacrament of Penance and Reconciliation? Or do we prefer a facile, lazy, and vague response of partial contrition for everything we are not in the light of his glory and perfection?

THIRD SUNDAY OF LENT—YEAR B

GOSPEL: JOHN 2:13-25

Meditation

Many wonder what provoked such a strong and virulent reaction from Jesus in today's passage, impelling him to make a whip of cords and drive out the merchants and money changers in the Temple precincts. The Jewish leaders had created a system of extortion whereby they forced pilgrims (who were coming to the Temple to offer the mandatory sacrifices for the High Holy Days) to buy the animals sold by the elders of the Temple. The prices (compared to what merchants in the rest of the city charged) were marked up nearly ten times, and the system greatly enriched the ruling class of Jerusalem. The guards at the gates of the Temple (hired by the elders) would not allow animals bought outside the precincts into the Temple area, thus forcing pilgrims to buy *their* products. (This situation was akin to how it is not permitted to bring in drinks from the outside beyond airport security, forcing passengers to buy drinks inside security and pay the markup in prices). Zeal for the Father's house filled Jesus with righteous anger, since he knew well how corrupt the elders had become, monetizing religion for their own gain. This cleansing of the Temple is often cited by scholars as one of the main reasons the ruling class sought to put Jesus to death.

Question(s) / Prayer

Do we have zeal for the Church? Do we have zeal for our parish? Are we indifferent to the community of faith in which we are planted, preferring a privatized experience of the Faith? Are we generous to the parish with our time, talent, and treasure? Do we do all we can to make sure that the parish acts with responsible stewardship towards the poor of our community? Does our zeal for the Father's house incentivize us to make frequent visits to the Blessed Sacrament individually and as a couple? In a world mired in hyper-individualism, zeal for the Father's house should motivate us to build community ties among fellow believers to build one another up in Christ.

THIRD SUNDAY OF LENT—YEAR C

GOSPEL: LUKE 13:1-9

Meditation

The second half of the gospel passage and the image of the unfruitful fig tree should serve as a poignant reminder that the Lord has high expectations of each of us as his faithful disciples. It is not enough to rest on one's laurels and to presume salvation. Instead, the Lord expects much more—and he warns us that time runs out, eventually. If we think that we can keep putting off spiritual growth and a serious and intentional discipleship, we fool ourselves into lethargy that will have dire consequences. The passage acknowledges that not all of us will be motivated by love. Sometimes, fear is enough to move someone out of apathy, with the hope that eventually love will become the motivation for fidelity and fruitfulness. Presumption is a dangerous spiritual malaise. Those who feel comfortable and accomplished in their lives but are not rich in what matters to God will face the precise outcome Jesus speaks of in today's passage. We ought to have ears to hear and eyes to see and perceive the things and people that God places before us to shake us out of our indifference. They will intercede for us . . . at least for a period of time. But eventually, time does run out on all of us.

Question(s) / Prayer

Father in heaven, help us to have ears to hear and eyes to see and perceive those signs that God places before us to shake us out of our indifference. May we not presume that we'll get to spiritual fruitfulness and discipleship later on in life. Help us to understand that now is the "acceptable time" and that now is the "day of salvation" (2 Cor 6:2). And as we strive for deeper conversion, grant us the fortitude to reach out to the many who we know suffer from the spiritual malaise of presumption and false comfort. May our sharing of our own experience of friendship with the Lord motivate others to become his friends too.

FOURTH SUNDAY OF LENT—YEAR A

GOSPEL: JOHN 9:1-41

Meditation

Today's gospel passage challenges us to consider physical blindness as a metaphor for spiritual blindness. The great paradox that the narrative reveals is that it is only when we acknowledge our spiritual blindness that we gain our sight. Analogously, the holier the saints seemed to other people to be becoming, the further the saints themselves realized they were from holiness. The man born blind does not make an appeal to Jesus for a cure, nor perhaps does he even realize that the Lord is walking by. In his mercy, the Lord cures him in such a way that draws out his faith and his willingness to give bold testimony to the Pharisees regarding his experience of Jesus. The self-righteous and self-assured Pharisees are the truly blind persons in the narrative. The faith-filled and humble man born blind ends up having true and clear vision because he assimilates the virtues that help transform his physical blindness into spiritual clarity. The man born blind was quite accustomed to living on the margins. He had lived his whole life as a beggar, and even after his cure, he remained on the margins—having been expelled from the synagogue. But from now on, his encounter with Jesus would change everything about his life, especially his capacity to see both exteriorly and interiorly.

Question(s) / Prayer

What are the blind spots in our marriage that we fail to acknowledge? Are we open to hearing honest but loving critiques from our spouse about areas where we can improve our capacity to love and relate to the other? Do we embrace with courage the challenge to acknowledge our deficits and how these may be a hindrance to our marital growth? Do we presume "to see" when in fact we are spiritually blind?

FOURTH SUNDAY OF LENT—YEAR B

GOSPEL: JOHN 3:14-21

Meditation

Jesus' words in today's Gospel are jarring. He states that "people preferred darkness to light" (Jn 3:19) even as he—the light of the world—has entered into human history to enlighten all minds and hearts with the love of the Father and faith in his Only-Begotten Son. Jesus goes on to call out those who preferred darkness to light precisely because their works were evil, "For everyone who does wicked things hates the light and does not come toward the light, so that his works might not be exposed" (Jn 3:20). By contrast, "whoever lives the truth comes to the light, so that his works may be clearly seen as done in God" (Jn 3:21). Everyone carries in them some darkness. This is not necessarily a darkness that needs to be revealed to one's spouse, but it must be brought to light in the confessional. That is perhaps the genius of the Sacrament of Penance—an offending spouse can confess their sins and resume their journey of discipleship without revealing those sins to their spouse that could forever ruin or end the marriage. The Lord so desires to heal and make marriages whole. Meanwhile, the Devil desires each of us to compromise on the truth about ourselves. We can give all the outward signs of being in step with the Lord, all the while carrying unresolved darkness that needs purification in the Sacrament of Penance. The confessional is the surest path to the interior freedom we all desire, so that we can be truly free to love God and others.

Question(s) / Prayer

Do we readily and regularly (i.e., every one to two months) confess our sins to a priest? Do we each take some time individually to make a brief but solid examination of conscience nightly? Are we sensitive to the state of our soul? Do we strive to be light for our spouse, especially if they are grappling with the darkness of their past or current life circumstances? Do we give them space and time and patience to work through their darkness so that we can help them to be free to love?

FOURTH SUNDAY OF LENT—YEAR C

GOSPEL: LUKE 15:1-3,11-32

Meditation

Perhaps the most famous of the parables, the story of the Prodigal Son reveals to us the Father's face of mercy. Lavish in his restoration of the wayward son to full status, his effusive mercy reaches beyond the strict measure of justice that can arise between two persons (even and perhaps especially between spouses) into a space of compassion that allows the injured person to enter into the world of the offending person to better understand the offense and its remedy. In a marriage, this compassion (literally, "to feel with") need not approve the way that the offending spouse has acted, but it reaches beyond the strict line of justice (what each is owed) so that reconciliation can begin. Forgiveness is a gift that spouses must learn to give one another, without any guarantee (or perhaps even expectation) of reciprocity. And this can only be done if one enters into the forgiveness the Father has for all sinners, for whom Jesus gave his life. The malcontent elder son in the parable has yet to enter into the Father's measure of mercy for the prodigal son. Rather, he is interested in strict justice, even complaining that he is implicitly owed some reward from the Father with which to celebrate with his friends. The Father reveals to us that mercy transcends strict justice—a virtue that married persons must cultivate in their relationship if it is to thrive.

Question(s) / Prayer

Lord, help each of us to apologize often, forgive quickly, and express our gratitude for the mercy our spouse has shown us. May we never take this spirit of compassion for granted if it already pervades the marriage. And if it does not, may we invite the Holy Spirit to fill us with the fortitude to not give in to pettiness and a strict measure of justice that subconsciously "keeps score" in the marriage, so that we can love with the heart of the Son.

FIFTH SUNDAY OF LENT—YEAR A

GOSPEL: JOHN 11:1-45

Meditation

Today's Gospel narrates the overwhelmingly dramatic resuscitation of Lazarus. This remarkable moment, witnessed by so many in Bethany, confirmed Jesus' divinity and accelerated his fame and notoriety, given that Jerusalem was so nearby. The event must have brought shock, wonderment, and pure awe and joy to those who experienced it first hand. Jesus' decision to wait four days before arriving in Bethany from Jerusalem was out of consideration for an ancient Jewish belief that the soul of the deceased lingered around the body for up to three days post mortem. Lazarus' resuscitation would have exceeded that three-day threshold, further demonstrating Jesus' power and substantiating his claim to be the Son of God, even before the Resurrection. But there's a verse in John's Gospel just beyond today's selection that is often overlooked: After witnessing this miracle, many of the Jewish elders sought to put Lazarus to death too, because he remained living proof of Jesus' claim to be exactly who he said he was (Jn 12:10). John is warning us too. Being the friends of Jesus is no easy task, and it can involve serious risks. If one is to live one's Catholic faith openly and without apology, one can expect opposition, mockery, and persecution.

Question(s) / Prayer

How prepared are we as individuals and as a couple to give open witness to the Lord? Do we cower in the face of opportunities to be like Lazarus—living proof of the grace of the Lord at work in the world? When people encounter us, do they give glory to God, like the witnesses of Lazarus' resuscitation? Are we all too ready to enjoy the consolation of friendship with Jesus privately without a real commitment to bearing witness to him publicly?

FIFTH SUNDAY OF LENT—YEAR B

GOSPEL: JOHN 12:20-33

Meditation

There's a wonderful progression of introduction and encounter in today's Gospel. John records that some Greeks were in Jerusalem for the Passover and desired to see Jesus. They go to Philip (one of the Apostles), whose Greek name suggests that he had some connection with Hellenistic (Greek) culture. Naturally, the Greeks go to someone with whom they can connect. Philip then approaches Andrew on their behalf, who himself is no stranger to introducing others (including his brother Peter) to the Lord. Together, Andrew and Philip bring these Greek converts to Judaism to the Lord. Notice what Jesus talks about upon meeting these Greeks. Rather than engage in warm, introductory pleasantries, Jesus' words are heavy—full of mysterious discourse about his death and his divine mission. He also indicates that all his disciples must learn to die to themselves and follow his self-emptying model of service. One can only imagine what type of impression the Lord made on these new acquaintances!

Question(s) / Prayer

Lord, help us to be conduits for others to encounter you in the fullness of what friendship with you entails. May we never hesitate to accompany those who are new to friendship with you, especially when that friendship seems demanding. Whenever your new friends are perplexed or feel overwhelmed by their newfound discipleship, may we offer support, consolation, and assurances that your plan for them is perfect. Grant us the grace to help them learn to trust you in all things, even as their witness and conversion to you inspires us.

FIFTH SUNDAY OF LENT—YEAR C

GOSPEL: JOHN 8:1-11

Meditation

Our most merciful Lord saves the sinful woman's life. She knows she owes her life to him. In the drama of this event, it is very easy to gloss over Jesus' precise instruction to the woman caught in adultery: "Go, [and] from now on, do not sin any more (Jn 8:11). In saving her life, Jesus does not approve of her sin. In fact, he calls her actions sinful. This should not be overlooked. This sense of sin is important for all disciples. And for all of recorded history, the human person has maintained a very strong sense of the need for God and of our estrangement from God, called sin. Postmodern society has lost all sense of this primordial reality. Throughout his pontificate, Pope Benedict XVI regularly observed that today, many live as if God does not exist. Postmoderns mistakenly believe that so long as they feel at peace with themselves, they are in God's good graces. But this is not necessarily the case. And the danger of this posture is that it implies that the subjective ego, not God, is the arbiter of all morality. And so God is replaced with the god of the self. If there is no sin, there is no need for Jesus. And if there is no need for Jesus?

Question(s) / Prayer

Father in heaven, help us to come to terms with the simple fact that we are sinners in need of the Lord, our Savior. May we recognize that we have blind spots that need healing, that we do not obey your moral law perfectly, and that we are in constant need of formation and moral conversion. May you inspire us to make frequent recourse to the Sacrament of Penance (Reconciliation) so that we might unite ourselves more perfectly to your Son's saving power and strive for the perfection he exhorts us to attain.

PALM SUNDAY OF THE LORD'S PASSION

GOSPEL: MATTHEW 26:14–27:66 (YEAR A) / MARK 14:1–15:47 (YEAR B) / LUKE 22:14–23:56 (YEAR C)

Meditation

St. Josemaría Escrivá, the founder of Opus Dei, had a habit of keeping a donkey figurine at his desk as a reminder of the donkey that bore our Lord into Jerusalem on Palm Sunday. The processing of a monarch on a donkey (versus a horse) into a city was considered a gesture of peacemaking (versus the conquering motif the use of a horse evoked). But the donkey itself often gets forgotten. This is precisely why St. Josemaría liked it so much—it reminded him of the vocation of a good disciple of Jesus. The donkey must bear in mind that the crowds cheering and singing *hosanna* on Palm Sunday aren't cheering for the donkey, but for the Lord. The donkey's role is to keep its head down, put one hoof in front of the other, and bear the Lord on its back for the world to see and adore. There is a humility in that role but one that keeps the disciple grounded in his mission, which is often hidden and known only to the Lord. In a world that over-glorifies celebrity status and attention-grabbing, the donkey is a wonderful reminder of who should truly reign in our lives—the Prince of Peace.

Question(s) / Prayer

Father in heaven, grant us the grace to be faithful donkeys for your son: simple, humble, and hidden. May we always be ready to deflect praise so that you are truly honored, and may we persevere in bearing your Son on our backs for all to see so that the world may know that he reigns in our hearts and that it is he who must be loved above all others.

HOLY THURSDAY—EVENING MASS OF THE LORD'S SUPPER

GOSPEL: JOHN 13:1-15

Meditation

At this Mass, the Church commemorates the institution of the Sacraments of Holy Orders and the Eucharist. Traditionally, priests and their bishop would gather in the morning for the celebration of the Chrism Mass, where the sacred oils for sacramental use were consecrated and the priests would renew their promises made at ordination. The evening Mass features the iconic scene in John 13—the washing of the feet, a ritual still performed in many places during this Mass. Christ's gesture towards his first bishops (the Twelve Apostles) was usually a work performed by a servant or slave. It is the epitome of humble, self-sacrificing service. Through it, the Lord inculcates in the Twelve his mind and heart regarding what it means to be great in his Kingdom. It is at once shocking and profoundly loving—the model for how spouses ought to love one another. In marriage, it is the daily act of the will to make the path for the other just a little easier and lighter. It is the spirit of loving in an anticipatory way, not merely going through the motions of daily life or having to be asked by the other for help. It is serving the other with humility and a gentle kindness, which can often be lost after the initial months and years of dating, courtship, engagement and the first months of marriage.

Question(s) / Prayer

Have we lost our initial servant's heart when it comes to anticipating the other's needs? Are we too busy "compromising" and "keeping score" when we should be more focused on giving without counting the cost? Do we relish outdoing the other in showing kindness and generosity? Would Christ recognize his love for us in the way we love one another in self-sacrificing and humble service? Do we ask, "What can I do or pray for today to lighten my spouse's load?"

GOOD FRIDAY OF THE LORD'S PASSION

GOSPEL: JOHN 18:1–19:42

Meditation

The Greek word *kenosis* captures one of the leading themes of the Passion narrative: self-emptying love. In the English-speaking world, today is known as Good Friday, which is quite paradoxical because it was a good day for everyone *but* Jesus. In complete self-abnegation, the Lord enters into all of human suffering (including every human emotion connected with it) and redeems it and makes it glorious and most meritorious. Jesus not only atones for all the sins of the world (past, present, future), he goes with us to the depths of every imaginable way human persons can and do suffer and lifts us out of that seemingly hopeless predicament by taking it upon himself. By taking on suffering, he reminds us that we cannot escape suffering in this life, in spite of every device or scheme we may invent to attempt it. And the depth of his love is not simply his willingness to endure the physical brutality that seems to distract us from the even greater suffering he felt in his human soul. This is known as Christ's moral suffering. It was not only the sense of complete abandonment by the Father but also the foreknowledge that for the many who would not accept him, all of his suffering would be ineffective. That is not to say that the Lord's suffering was deficient. But it does mean that if the human person is unwilling to believe in him and follow him, the merits of redemption will not save him.

Question(s) / Prayer

Lord, help us to break out of the indifference into which we can fall when we take our eyes off of you. When we doubt your love for us and the power of the Cross, inspire us to spend time in front of a crucifix meditating upon what you accomplished for us. Help us to recall that you purchased for us that which none of us could garner for ourselves—victory over sin and eternal death. Help us to reprioritize our lives so as to place the Cross and the response of love that it demands at the center of our lives. We are so easily distracted from the decisiveness that the Cross beckons us to, placing so many unimportant things ahead of our discipleship. May your Cross move us to repentance and love for you.

EASTER SUNDAY—THE RESURRECTION OF THE LORD

GOSPEL: JOHN 20:1-9

Meditation

St. John's account of the empty tomb contains remarkable details about the status of the burial cloths and the head cloth that covered the Lord's head in the tomb. A growing number of scholars contend that John was trying to communicate that the Lord *passed through the cloths* and that SS. John and Peter found them in a deflated form. And it was upon seeing this reality that St. John believed. In subsequent scenes depicting the risen Lord interacting with the disciples, we will discover that Jesus' resurrected state is not a mere resuscitated state. A resuscitated body (like that of Lazarus or Jairus's daughter or the son of the widow of Naim) would die again. The Lord's resurrected body will never die, and John's description of it seems to indicate that the Lord entered a fourth dimension of reality, never seen before. But more than just a theological or scientific curiosity, the resurrected state points to a deeper truth: It is the pattern for how we will experience the life of the world to come in all glory (heaven, perhaps preceded by Purgatory) or all condemnation (hell). But it also reminds us how Jesus got there—through the portal of Good Friday. Suffering and agony lead to the hope of the empty tomb!

Question(s) / Prayer

Father in heaven, help us to have our sights on heaven! May we learn the science of the Cross, which leads to the hope of the empty tomb. But may we never presume our salvation. Help us to own our path to glory, but not with merely earthly eyes that reduce the glory of the resurrected state to some man-made manufactured facsimile. Rather, help us to have the eyes of faith to understand why our supernatural destiny moved St. Paul to marvel at

> What eye has not seen, and ear has not heard,
> and what has not entered the human heart,
> what God has prepared for those who love him. (1 Cor 2:9)

SECOND SUNDAY OF EASTER—DIVINE MERCY SUNDAY

GOSPEL: JOHN 20:19-31

Meditation

Jesus' offer of peace to the Apostles on Easter Sunday night was such a significant moment for them. Recall that the last time that Jesus and the Apostles were together was on Holy Thursday night in the Garden of Gethsemane. That evening ended in utter catastrophe. Jesus was arrested and all of the Apostles (except St. John) fled. In a matter of hours, the first pope had denied the Lord three times and Judas Iscariot had hung himself. St. John's rendition of Easter Sunday night indicates that the Apostles were hiding in the upper room for fear of the Jews. It's not too speculative to say that they might have been hiding in the upper room for fear of Jesus. We can imagine how embarrassed, crestfallen, and guilt-ridden they must have felt when they first saw the risen Lord. But Jesus' peace quickly turned their sorrow and devastation to joy. His offer of peace said to the Apostles: I am not here to condemn but to forgive. I am not here to berate but to console. I am not here to find fault but to heal. The Lord transcends sin, suffering, and eternal death.

Question(s) / Prayer

Lord, whenever we want to give in to bickering, pettiness, and an unloving attitude, help us to recall your offer of peace to your Apostles. Help us to imitate you by rising above the exacting of mere justice and reaching over the line of justice into the realm of mercy. May we be slow to accuse, quick to apologize, and even quicker to forgive. May our commitment to a paradigm of mercy, reconciliation, and understanding create an ambiance of mildness, humility, and joy.

THIRD SUNDAY OF EASTER—YEAR A

GOSPEL: LUKE 24:13-35

Meditation

Still basking in the glory of Easter Sunday, the Church presents us with the story of the Road to Emmaus, which occurred on Easter Sunday night. Contained within the narrative is the pattern for the Holy Sacrifice of the Mass. Notice that the first part of the encounter with Jesus is a Liturgy of the Word (Jesus opens up the Scriptures for the two disciples). The second part (the breaking of the bread) is a Liturgy of the Eucharist. And notice how the two "liturgies" heal this pair of abject and disoriented disciples, who are first encountered walking away from Jerusalem (symbolizing heaven). Once they recognize the Lord, they immediately set out to return in the right direction (towards Jerusalem)! They even recount how their hearts were burning as Jesus opened the Word to them. This is what ought to happen for us at the Mass—we should leave the experience re-oriented towards heaven, having come to Mass from a disoriented and vexing world. The Mass is meant to heal us too if we have eyes to recognize its power.

Question(s) / Prayer

What are the dispositions we bring to Mass? Is it the highlight of our Sunday, or is Sunday just another day in the larger "weekend mentality" that pervades the secular culture around us? Is Sunday about allowing our hearts to burn with love for the Lord, or is it more about the big game on TV or the sports competitions of the children? What must we do to recapture Sunday as the Lord's Day, and how can we approach the Mass and its healing power with the right dispositions?

THIRD SUNDAY OF EASTER—YEAR B
GOSPEL: LUKE 24:35-48

Meditation

Still basking in the glory of Easter Sunday, the Church presents us with the continuation of the story of the Road of Emmaus, which occurred on Easter Sunday night. Here Luke recounts the first time the Lord appeared to the eleven Apostles after the Resurrection. His words are curative: "Peace be with you" (Lk 24:36). We must not underestimate how much the Apostles needed to hear those healing words. Recall that the last time they were all together in that upper room was the Last Supper. And we know well how the next hours were totally disastrous for them, in spite of the fact that they had all sworn to stay with Jesus in his hour of need. Jesus' offer of peace said so much to them: that Jesus had conquered death and sin, including their betrayal of him.

Luke also includes painstaking details regarding Jesus' resurrected body. The Lord asks to eat a piece of baked fish in front of the Apostles, reminding them that he is not a ghost but has a true human body and true human soul, albeit in a glorified state, which transcends anything anyone had ever seen before. This integration of Jesus' body and soul reminds us that salvation involves both of these dimensions of our existence. In other words, it is not simply our souls that are saved—the reunification of our bodies with our souls at the resurrection of the body is a credal statement that we affirm weekly at Sunday Mass and that is essential to our salvation from damnation. Hence, what we do with our bodies affects our souls, as we are body-soul composites. But thanks be to

God that the Resurrected One has elevated our dignity to new heights and made us capable of living a life of integrated virtue.

*Question(s) / **Prayer***

Lord, help us to remember that our bodies are temples of the Holy Spirit and that we are called to live chastity in our marriage. May we always act and speak in ways that give you glory and honor and remain faithful to the promises we made on our wedding day. Might your resurrected body remind us of our eternal destiny and that our salvation consists in being saved in body and soul. Help us to remember that what we do writes the story of who we become and that it is your grace that sustains us in living lives worthy of the calling we have received.

THIRD SUNDAY OF EASTER—YEAR C

GOSPEL: JOHN 21:1-19

Meditation

St. Augustine reminds us that Jesus asks Peter thrice, "Do you love me?" as a remedy for Peter's triple denial of Jesus on Holy Thursday night. But there is another way to understand this exchange. In Greek, the first two times Jesus asks Peter, "Do you love me?" he uses the form of the word "love" connected with *agape*, which is unconditional love. This is often associated with the love that a parent has for their child. And twice Peter's response uses the form of the word "love" connected with *philia*, which is brotherly or intellectual love (Jn 21:15-16). In other words, Peter cannot match the Lord's love for him. In the third instance, Jesus asks Peter if Peter's love is *philia*. This is what hurts Peter—that the Lord has shown him that Peter's love isn't what Jesus expects: *agape*. Peter's response is telling. He says, "Lord, you know everything; you know that I love (*philia*) you" (Jn 21:17). Happily, Peter would have another chance to show the Lord his love (*agape*), when he died as a martyr in Rome in about the year AD 64. It is remarkable to consider that perhaps the exchange in today's Gospel came to Peter's mind as he was about to endure his martyrdom, some thirty years after the Resurrection. Perhaps he may have felt a great deal of gratitude for another chance to prove his love for the Lord. There is an evolution within every marriage. What perhaps was first dominated by *eros* (the love of the marital embrace or a love that pursues the beloved in order to possess them), can change over time on account of age, health, or life circumstances.

Question(s) / Prayer

How do we cultivate love in our marriage? For the Lord? For our children? Does our love also include a readiness to forgive and heal, just as Jesus healed Peter's triple denial? Do we anticipate each other in showing love, always seeking ways to make the path of the other just a bit easier to bear? How do we express our love in ways that make the other feel loved, cherished, and valued?

FOURTH SUNDAY OF EASTER

GOSPEL: JOHN 10:1-10 (YEAR A) / JOHN 10:11-18 (YEAR B) / JOHN 10:27-30 (YEAR C)

Meditation

The Fourth Sunday of Easter is also known as Good Shepherd Sunday, a day typically dedicated to promoting vocations to the priesthood and religious life, since the image of the Good Shepherd evokes images of the pastoral care of God's people, especially through the ministry of priests. The gospel passages today are not only about the need to be led by the Good Shepherd (so necessary in an era of self-assertiveness and unwillingness to be led), but also about the need to have the ear to discern the Lord's voice, which competes with so many false prophets of our time. For married couples, it also raises the challenge of promoting vocations to the priesthood and religious life in their families. Dioceses all have programs to promote vocations, but vocations come from families first and foremost. It is in the family, the domestic church, that children learn about and can consider God's call. But in so many sectors of the Church today, the idea of pursuing a vocation to the priesthood or religious life today is almost impossible to cultivate because such a calling is considered an oddity or because whole families are not practicing the Faith. The crisis is never one of God not calling enough men to the priesthood or enough men or women to the religious life. The crisis is one of generous response. The family is the typical seedbed for this response.

Question(s) / Prayer

Do we value and treasure consecrated celibacy for the sake of the Kingdom as an objectively higher calling than marriage, or do we place "pressure" on our children to produce grandchildren, as if our children and potential grandchildren are our possessions? Do we cultivate a culture of vocations in our home, where children can pursue the noble calling to the priesthood and religious life with joy and freedom? Do we speak well of clergy, so that they are esteemed in our home? Are they welcomed as guests? Do we pray for vocations generically, but fear the possibility that one of our own family members is called? What does this say about our faith or lack thereof?

FIFTH SUNDAY OF EASTER—YEAR A

GOSPEL: JOHN 14:1-12

Meditation

Jesus' words to his disciples signify a massive paradigm shift for men who were raised as believing Jews. Recall that for the Jews, God was so foreign and so "other" that the concept of God becoming man was a massive departure from anything they had known or believed previously. Jesus says that no one comes to the Father except through him, that he is the way, the truth, and the life (Jn 14:6) and that he who sees the Lord has seen the Father (Jn 14:9). While we take these statements and ideas for granted, they would have been quite stunning for the disciples to hear. And Jesus is not speaking in allegorical or metaphorical terms. He literally means what he says, and his words open up a new horizon for his followers. They compelled the early Church Fathers to say and write repeatedly that God became man so that man could become like God, a concept known as deification. This is the depth of what Jesus is about. He is not simply a spiritual guru or sage. He is God's Only-Begotten Son, who opened for us unprecedented access to the Father. He does not demand obedience to his teachings so much as he requires faith in him, personally and to the core of one's being. When the act of faith matures, obedience to his teachings follows naturally.

Question(s) / Prayer

Lord, help us to enter into a communion of faith in you. May we avoid the temptation to reduce you to a lawgiver or spiritual guide, but rather enter deeply into relationship with you, so much so that we regard a life without you as a type of death. Grant us the grace of a radical conversion to you, so that every thought, word, and deed of ours may begin with you and through you reach its happy completion.

FIFTH SUNDAY OF EASTER—YEAR B

GOSPEL: JOHN 15:1-8

Meditation

At first glance, the image of the vine and the branches can appear innocuous, even romantic. After all, who doesn't like visiting a vineyard and partaking in a wine tasting? But a closer examination of the image reveals Jesus' vision for discipleship. Jesus indicates that he is the vine, and we are the branches. And yet how easy is it to live as if we are the vine and Jesus is the branch! In other words, the Lord wants us to know who exactly is God in relation to us—God himself, or us? Jesus also states that he will cut away and burn all those branches that do not bear fruit. And he goes even further: those who do bear fruit get pruned (a metaphor for suffering) so that they can become even more fruitful and robust branches. Suddenly, the romance of the image is lost. Jesus reminds us that we are to abide in him and that without him we can do nothing. If we are not prepared to be a branch on the vine that is the Lord, we will eventually wither and perish. The image of the vine and branches doesn't include any mention of the various conditions that promote growth, such as a gentle breeze, optimal temperature and humidity, and adequate moisture. These are the conditions needed for the vine to grow and flourish. By extension, this image compels us to consider the type of conditions we invite into our marriage and family in order to promote sanctity and authentic love.

Question(s) / Prayer

We claim that Jesus is the vine and we are the branches, but are our lives qualitatively different from those of our secular peers? Do we promote the proper conditions so that we can abide in the Lord? Is Jesus truly the vine in our marriage, or is it in fact the case that we are the vine and Jesus is just an accessory to our lives? Do we see the suffering we bear as the Father's gentle pruning, which often breaks through the barrier of our spiritual deafness and reorients us back to him?

FIFTH SUNDAY OF EASTER—YEAR C

GOSPEL: JOHN 13:31-33A, 34-35

Meditation

Jesus' command to his disciples that they should love one another as Christ has loved them (Jn 13:34) is a necessary elixir in a world where the common mantra "Love is love" reigns supreme. Love and freedom can never be separated from the truth, who is Christ himself (the way, the truth, and the life (Jn 14:6)). Christian love is bound up in obedience to God's moral law—a self-sacrificing love that puts love of God above all other loves. It is a love that bears wrongs patiently, that seeks the good of one's enemies, that is ordered and effusive and never counts the cost. All genuine human love is a participation in God's love for the human person and therefore demands conformity to his will. Any claim to love that does not respect God's moral law loses its proper use and goal and easily becomes perverted and self-seeking. It is Christ crucified who teaches us to love truly.

Question(s) / Prayer

Is our marital and family love well ordered? Do we place love of God above all? Do other "loves" compete for the love we ought to have for the Lord as our first priority? Do we see that it is only when we love as Christ has commanded us that we love authentically? Do we understand that any definition of love that we concoct that is not in conformity with God (who is love) loses its way, no matter how well-intending it may be? What must we do to rediscover the proper orientation our love for one other must have?

SIXTH SUNDAY OF EASTER—YEAR A

GOSPEL: JOHN 14:15-21

Meditation

In preparation for his glorious Ascension, the Lord promises to send the Holy Spirit to dwell in the hearts of his followers. He refers to the Holy Spirit as "the Spirit of truth, whom the world cannot accept, because it neither sees nor knows it" (Jn 14:17). This is a very serious warning if one heeds it closely. The Lord is explicitly alerting his followers that following him will put them in stark opposition to the spirit of the world, which is wounded by sin, division, and corruption. And this is the challenge of living a life in the Holy Spirit: to live in the world without adopting its spirit. It's a challenge to use the things of the world as means to spiritual perfection (personal holiness) and not as ends unto themselves. And yet most persons who try to follow Christ fail repeatedly, and at times fatally, when it comes to adopting this approach to life. The true disciple interprets the spirit of the world accurately, without compromise, and lives steadfastly according to the Lord's commands. It is no wonder that the passage concludes with Jesus' statement, "Whoever has my commandments and observes them is the one who loves me. And whoever loves me will be loved by my Father, and I will love him and reveal myself to him" (Jn 14:21).

Question(s) / Prayer

Are we prepared to take a thorough and honest look at how much the spirit of the world influences us? Do we have the Spirit of truth, or do we prefer to relative comfort of living lives that please the pervading spirit of the world? Do we claim discipleship but live it on our terms? Or do we live in the Spirit of truth and accept his crosses and blessings?

SIXTH SUNDAY OF EASTER—YEAR B

GOSPEL: JOHN 15:9-17

Meditation

Jesus says, "You are my friends if you do what I command you. I no longer call you slaves, because a slave does not know what his master is doing. I have called you friends, because I have told you everything I have heard from my Father. It was not you who chose me, but I who chose you and appointed you to go and bear fruit that will remain… (Jn 15:12-16). The Lord offers us a remarkable type of friendship. He says that we are his friends if (and only if) we keep his commandments. So the Lord offers us friendship, but not as a peer or equal offers us friendship. This is a unique and qualified friendship, since it involves the Lord, who is capable of saving us—a quality no other friend we can have possesses. And while this friendship grants us unprecedented access to the Father, it also demands that we bear fruit for the Lord. As if the Apostles hadn't already had enough to grasp in assimilating the reality that God had become man in the person of Jesus—they then discover that the God-Man offers them life-giving friendship unto salvation. Truly remarkable. It can be said that there are two types of people on earth: his friends (who obey his commands) and his foes (those who ignore or disobey him). There is no middle ground. Every person who encounters the Lord must make this decision daily—to be or not to be his friend on the terms he sets.

Question(s) / Prayer

How do we understand friendship with Christ? Is it a friendship based on obedience to the Lord, or a friendship shaped by our standards and expectations? Do we realize how much we forfeit by not entering into friendship with the Lord, or do we prefer to go our own way, seeking our own definition of happiness and contentment? Is the Lord a friend of convenience—one to whom we turn whenever needs arise? Or is the Lord our most intimate friend, who knows us through and through and to whom we turn always? How is our marriage oriented towards friendship in Christ? Is he central to our relationship or a mere accessory?

SIXTH SUNDAY OF EASTER—YEAR C

GOSPEL: JOHN 14:23-29

Meditation

Most couples and families place a premium on "keeping the peace" when conflicts brew. And in many cases, most people can be satisfied with relationships as long as there is no open "warfare." And yet this reductionist view of peace does not meet the standard of the peace that Christ promises. He says, "Peace I leave with you; my peace I give to you. Not as the world gives do I give it to you" (Jn 14:27). What does Christian peace look like? In sum, Christian peace is not the mere absence of conflict. Rather, Christian peace is borne out of the presence of justice (simply, giving others what they are owed) in relationships. In other words, peace is the fruit of justice. And how does justice become a reality? Justice means apologizing and forgiving. It means bending the will toward the other out of love and a desire for the will of God to reign supreme. And peace can flourish where mercy abounds. Mercy reaches beyond the line of strict justice into a space of mutual understanding and empathy. It is accompanied by an agreeableness that sees beyond what are often petty disagreements. The evil one loves division, rancor, and selfishness. Jesus loves unity, mildness, and generosity. These are key ingredients in flourishing marriages and families.

Question(s) / Prayer

Are we true peacemakers or just conflict avoiders? Do we allow the wounds of injustice to fester? Do we seek a justice rooted in the objective truth of the Gospel or some unreasonable and invented form of justice that merely suits our whims? Do we "fight fair"—that is, do we avoid making recourse to hurtful, disproportionate, and illogical arguments in order to win an argument when we really know that "winning" is often just a larger part of losing one's spouse? Do we work at creating a space of patient forbearance and compassion?

SOLEMNITY OF THE ASCENSION OF THE LORD

GOSPEL: MATTHEW 28:16-20 (YEAR A) / MARK 16:15-20 (YEAR B) / LUKE 24:46-53 (YEAR C)

Meditation

All three accounts of the Ascension feature the evangelical/ missionary orientation of the Church. In other words, the Lord always had in mind the preaching of the Gospel to the nations as constitutive of the Church's very nature. The Lord never intended the Church he founded to be a private club or a hotel for the saved. Rather, he has always desired a Church that reaches out to the peripheries and converts the multitudes to the Gospel. If every family is a domestic church, the mission of the family should be the same: evangelical. It is not enough that families practice the faith and grow in holiness *ad intra*. Instead, families are to reach out to others *ad extra* to help them encounter Christ and the Church in all of its life-giving splendor. Unfortunately, most "Catholic" families today fail to reach the first standard of holiness *ad intra*. This hampers *ad extra* evangelization. And yet, how inspirational it can be when one encounters a dynamic and intentionally evangelical family—joyful in their apostolate and vibrant in their love for one another. The Church needs a revitalization of the Catholic family, which lies dormant in most regions of the world today.

Question(s) / Prayer

How do we foster the missionary orientation of the Church within our family? Is personal and family holiness a priority? Do our deficits *ad intra* hamper our efforts *ad extra*? Are we credible witnesses to the Resurrection and Ascension of the Lord? What are small steps we can take to animate the Faith among us?

SEVENTH SUNDAY OF EASTER—YEAR A

(where the Solemnity of the Ascension is celebrated on the prior Thursday)

GOSPEL: JOHN 17:1-11A

Meditation

Jesus says, "Now this is eternal life, that they should know you, the only true God, and the one whom you sent, Jesus Christ" (Jn17:4). Biblical knowledge connotes intimacy. For instance, in the Book of Genesis, we read how Adam "knew" Eve (Gn 4:1, Douay-Rheims). Jesus desires us to have divine intimacy with the Trinity—to enter into communion with the triune God. This communion is not so much about our efforts to know God, but rather about being known by him. This communion requires docility, an open heart, and a sincere desire to orient one's life to God in all things. This is the intimacy that the saints experienced. They allowed themselves to be "found" or "known" by God in such a way that they no longer lived for themselves but for him who died for them. Entering into this intimacy requires the virtue of courage, for it often compels the human person who wishes to be known by God to move beyond their comfort zone and into a "riskier" space of abandonment to divine providence. By analogy, this "risk" is what married persons seek of one another—to be "known" to the other in one's vulnerabilities and insecurities and to be loved in spite of one's deficits. This is a sacred intimacy that couples experience when they are truly connected, and it finds its pattern and source in God's seeking out of the human person.

Question(s) / Prayer

Lord, help us to foster this sacred space of intimacy in our marriage with a true spirit of charity, mildness, mercy, compassion, and fidelity. Help us to have the courage to be known by the other and to be known by you, who desire to imbue each of us with your Spirt, individually and as a couple. May we put aside all posturing, gamesmanship, compromises, and rationalizations whenever we are tempted to put up obstacles to the intimacy we need and desire. Help us to trust in the power and efficacy of divine mercy, which never fails, even when marital attempts falter.

SEVENTH SUNDAY OF EASTER—YEAR B

(where the Solemnity of the Ascension is celebrated on the prior Thursday)

GOSPEL: JOHN 17:11B-19

Meditation

In his prayer to the Father, Jesus says, "I gave them your word, and the world hated them, because they do not belong to the world any more than I belong to the world. I do not ask that you take them out of the world but that you keep them from the evil one. They do not belong to the world any more than I belong to the world" (Jn 17:14-16). Traditionally, the three enemies of the soul are the world, the flesh, and the Devil. Here, Jesus prays for the preservation of his disciples from two of these three enemies (world and Devil). One may ask, "What is 'the world' of which Jesus speaks?" The "world" is a spirit of worldliness—a spirit of self-sufficiency (versus biblical dependency on God), a spirit of arrogance and pride that sets its own terms for virtue and the path to salvation ("I'll be saved so long as I am essentially a 'good' person according to my standards"), and a spirit of spiritual laziness or boredom (*acedia*) that refuses to embrace the Spirit and a life of personal holiness. Sadly, an increasing number of Catholics today have embraced the spirit of the world, preferring to be loved by the worldly. It manifests itself in the massive decline in Church attendance on Sundays and Holy Days, and a quasi-Catholic morality espoused by those who pick and choose the moral teachings of the Church that suit their lifestyles best. Catholics are called to live in the world but not to adopt its spirit. True discipleship means excelling in all things and imbuing everything with the spirt of the Gospel.

Question(s) / Prayer

In our marriage, are we governed by the spirit of the world? Do worldly values inform and guide our moral decision-making? Are we that different from our secular counterparts, or do we mostly imitate them, save an occasional prayer or thought of God? What are we prepared to change in our lives in order to adopt the Spirit of the Lord?

SEVENTH SUNDAY OF EASTER—YEAR C

(where the Solemnity of the Ascension is celebrated on the prior Thursday)

GOSPEL: JOHN 17:20-26

Meditation

Jesus' prayer for unity has serious implications for married couples, and not in the obvious sense. Jesus' prayer for unity is based on living a life rooted in Christ, while respecting that each spouse remains a separate person capable of making decisions that may be at variance with the other's. In other words, spousal unity does not mean that the spouses collapse into each other without retaining their individuality. In regard to a unity based on living a life rooted in Christ, this means that the couple remains unified through the lens of the Christian life. After all, a couple may be unified in their common desire to commit sin. Sure, the couple may be unified, but their unity is illusory since it is not rooted in human flourishing and the spouses' eternal destiny in heaven. Hence, true unity can never be separated from the truth of the Gospel. At times, one spouse may be willing to tempt the other into sin using the excuse of spousal "unity." But this would be a false unity since it is rooted in a lie. And it is the Father of Lies (Satan), who loves this type of "unity." One need no look any farther than Genesis 3 and story of Original Sin to understand how the Evil One used a "unity" outside of God's plan to wreak havoc on the human family. Adam and Eve were united, but their "unity" introduced sin and its division into the world.

Question(s) / Prayer

Lord, help us to examine and re-examine the source for our spousal unity. Are we united in our common love for you? Do we foster a unity that is life-giving and virtuous, or one that is selfish and rooted in vice? Are we quick to conflate a false "unity" with the genuine unity you desire for us, simply because we feel good about our alleged "unity"? Do we possess the self-awareness to admit that our alleged "unity" may quite divisive, because it alienates us from the Lord?

PENTECOST SUNDAY

GOSPEL: JOHN 20:19-23

Meditation

On this last day of Eastertide, today's Gospel takes us back to Easter Sunday night, the beginning of Eastertide. It's as if this reading serves as an appropriate set of bookends for the liturgical celebration of the last fifty days. In a dramatic gesture, Jesus breathes on his disciples as he says, "Receive the Holy Spirit" (Jn 20:22). This form of the word "breathe" is identical to the version of the word found in Genesis 2:7, when God breathed life into the body of Adam. John's Gospel wants us to connect the creation of man with the creation of the Church. It evokes the generative work of the Holy Spirit, which animates and vivifies the life of the Church—from the efficacy of the sacraments to the inspirations that have led to the manifold charisms and movements within the Church and the lives of sanctity of our canonized saints. As a sacrament, marriage is animated by the promptings of the Holy Spirit. Couples do well to invoke the power of the Holy Spirit to fortify, heal, preserve, and grow their marriage. So often, couples think that their fruitfulness is contingent on *their* efforts merely. The reality is quite the opposite—it's much more dependent on a receptivity to the movements of the Spirit. Reducing or eliminating blockages to these movements may be the crucial nexus point between God's inner workings and a couple's efforts, and even these promptings to eliminate or reduce blockages are moved by the Spirit.

Question(s) / Prayer

What prevents the Spirit from animating our marriage? Do we truly believe that our spiritual fruitfulness is contingent upon the work of the Spirit, or do we tend to think that the Spirit is only needed when our personal resources are lacking? Do we pray to the Holy Spirit to fortify, heal, preserve, and strengthen our bond? If the sacraments are the normative way in which we encounter God's inner life, can we say that our marriage reflects this reality?

SUNDAYS IN ORDINARY TIME— YEAR A

SECOND SUNDAY IN ORDINARY TIME—YEAR A

GOSPEL: JOHN 1:29-34

Meditation

Today's Gospel narrates the events of the Lord's Baptism in the Jordan River, the template for Christian Baptism, which is the sacrament most necessary for salvation. The Baptism that the Church confers is the most fundamental sacrament, and its recipient receives the indwelling of the Holy Trinity by sanctifying grace; the three theological virtues of faith, hope and charity; the seven gifts of the Holy Spirit; and the cleansing of Original Sin and actual sins (for those who receive the sacrament after the age of reason—normally seven years old). As a sacrament, Holy Matrimony specifies the way a believer is to live out his or her baptismal dignity as priest (sanctification), prophet (teaching), and king (governing). The other sacrament of vocation is Holy Orders. Both sacraments are oriented to living out one's baptismal dignity and vocation in a particular manner. These basic realities demonstrate the Lord's mercy for us—that in order to live out our baptismal call to holiness, he gives us two more sacraments to live that general call in a specific way.

Question(s) / Prayer

How seriously do I take the universal call to holiness, conferred upon me at Baptism? Does our marriage have holiness as a priority? Do we understand that holiness does not always mean mere emotional bliss, which is often the superficial goal for many couples? Lord, help us to plumb the depths of our baptismal call by inspiring us to be well-catechized about both this sacrament and the Sacrament of Marriage. May we always recall that our marriage is not just about our relationship with each other, but it is first about our relationship with you. And it is this relationship that informs and guides our relationship with each other.

THIRD SUNDAY IN ORDINARY TIME—YEAR A
GOSPEL: MATTHEW 4:12-23

Meditation

The central message of the preaching of Jesus is contained in today's Gospel: Repent, for the Kingdom of Heaven is at hand! Repentance is not merely moral conversion. Rather, repentance entails a re-prioritization of one's life. It ranges from the dramatic to the subtle re-orientation of one's life to Christ. Moral conversion flows from this fundamental refocusing. Moral conversion is usually a sign of repentance, but its roots should run much deeper. This is precisely the re-prioritization that took place in the lives of the Apostles, also featured in today's Gospel. They left their former way of life and embarked on a profoundly new life in Christ. This repentance has to happen time and again in marriage. With so many seemingly important things (most are illusory, if we are honest) pulling at us and vying for our attention, we are in constant need to re-prioritize a life in Christ. This is marked by a more intentional discipleship rooted in serious prayer, complete participation in the sacraments, study of the Faith, and growth in virtue. It requires dying to the old self and beginning anew in Christ. In this model, Christ is no longer once of many voices we merely consume, like a favorite podcast or YouTube channel. Rather, he becomes the central protagonist in our lives so that it is no longer the "I" who lives, but Christ who lives in me. Attempting to start with moral conversion, instead of a fundamental re-orientation of one's life to Christ, is usually short-lived. Hence, repentance rooted in faith in the Lord is the all-important priority.

Question(s) / Prayer

Where are the areas of our married life that still require genuine repentance? Do we assume that moral conversion is the starting point, or do we more fully grasp the depth of authentic repentance—rooted in faith and friendship with the Lord? Are we prepared to make those necessary re-prioritizations and re-orientations so that Christ truly reigns in our hearts? What are the concrete ways in which this faith-based repentance can start to take shape in our marriage?

FOURTH SUNDAY IN ORDINARY TIME—YEAR A

GOSPEL: MATTHEW 5:1-12A

Meditation

The Beatitudes are the cornerstone and foundation of the entire Christian moral life. While the Ten Commandments express the natural law in the language of divine revelation, the Beatitudes constitute that infinite horizon tending towards Christian perfection. And yet most Catholics give them little thought when they confess their sins. And even more Catholics treat the Beatitudes like biblical fortune cookie sayings! In other words, the Beatitudes present aspirations, but they are completely out of reach. Nothing could be more untrue! The Beatitudes are the key to experiencing the interior freedom that Jesus desires for each human person. Some theologians believe that the Beatitudes represent the portrait of Jesus himself. And if we are to be *Christ*ians, we must aspire to all they demand in order to experience their promise.

Question(s) / Prayer

Heavenly Father, assist us with your grace to learn the Beatitudes by heart and to have them always before us (perhaps hung on a wall in our home) so that they may be the pattern and goal of how we live as your disciples. May our marriage and family life be outward expressions of the interior virtues that the Beatitudes express. Help us to see that the Beatitudes both challenge us to conversion and console us in our trials, as we try to live out your life in us.

FIFTH SUNDAY IN ORDINARY TIME—YEAR A

GOSPEL: MATTHEW 5:13-16

Meditation

The images of salt and light connote the evangelical spirit that Jesus indicates his followers must have in order to be true disciples. Salt isn't meant to sit in a saltshaker. Rather, its value is realized when it seasons or preserves food. And salt must retain its saltiness in order to demonstrate its value. That is not to say that we ought to be "salty" evangelizers who manifest an acerbic spirit. Instead, it suggests that as evangelizers, we cannot allow our faith to grow dull, lest we have nothing to offer others. It must be cultivated by prayer, study, and good works.

Similarly, Jesus envisions light dispersing darkness and spreading itself all over a house, not to be kept under a bushel basket. A light kept hidden fails to accomplish its purpose: illumination. Put another way, salt and light are images that indicate the need for us to engage others through our marriage and the network of relationships that it touches. How edifying it is to see couples get together for social occasions, which also serve as moments to share one couple's friendship with Christ in a spirit of naturalness and with good cheer! If the Gospel is in fact Good News, truly apostolic couples won't be able to keep it under wraps for long.

Question(s) / Prayer

Is our faith too private? Does it have an outward trajectory? Are we too uneasy to show or share that dimension of our lives with others? Does our home contain outward signs that communicate to guests that Jesus reigns supreme? Are we embarrassed by our faith, or are we perhaps overbearing with it? Does our marriage demonstrate the peace, spiritual intimacy, and depth that Christ desires so much for us? Or have we grown cold, indifferent, and materialistic, so that the spirit of the Gospel is a mere afterthought?

SIXTH SUNDAY IN ORDINARY TIME—YEAR A
GOSPEL: MATTHEW 5:17-37

Meditation

In this very lengthy passage, Jesus brings up the question of divorce and remarriage. Of all the moral teachings he proffers, Jesus goes into the most detail on this precise question. If one were to examine the other places in the Gospels where Jesus discusses divorce and remarriage, it is clear that he is returning us to the creation accounts in Genesis about the indissolubility of the marriage bond. Jesus is not just saying that divorce is sinful—he's saying it's simply not possible. That is why the annulment process is the Church ought not to be called "Catholic divorce." A divorce is the declaration of a civil court that a marital contract once existed and has been terminated. An annulment declaration states that at the time marriage was attempted, no valid marriage was established. (This has no impact on the "legitimacy" of the children born out of the union, since these are matters decided by the civil court.) Given the high divorce rate (more than 50 percent in the US), couples need to guard against every possible temptation to abandon the union that has been established in the sacramental covenant between a husband and wife. Earlier in this passage, Jesus uses the hyperboles of gouging out one's eye and severing one's hand rather than risk eternal perdition. The same could be true of the marriage. Every effort to cultivate, preserve, and assist the marriage covenant and the spiritual closeness of intimacy must be taken.

Question(s) / Prayer

Lord, grant us the perseverance and fortitude necessary to grow together in our marriage. May we be willing to amputate all those things in our lives that hinder us from remaining truly united and connected to you and to one another. Even when we have disagreements and fights, may we never allow resentment to fester, but resolve things quickly and graciously, so as to prevent the division that the Devil relishes. May we never play into his hands, but place our hands firmly in the grasp of your loving embrace, knowing that you desire us to be one in heart and affections.

SEVENTH SUNDAY IN ORDINARY TIME—YEAR A

GOSPEL: MATTHEW 5:38-48

Meditation

Jesus' command to love one's enemies and to reject the ancient maxim of "an eye for an eye" would have been extremely controversial to his hearers. Both Judaism and Islam remain "eye for an eye" moral systems—perhaps one of the reasons why they have been at war in the Holy Land for so long. Christian love proffers a third way: the moderation that mercy and forgiveness bring. Forgiveness is an essential dimension of marital love. While spouses can bring each other immense happiness, spouses can also cause great annoyance and frustration, not to mention devastating pain. To be fruitful in their marriage, couples must commit to cease all bickering the moment it starts and to take time apart to cool off and then to make amends. It is sad to observe couples who have lost their way and now hold one another in contempt. Unresolved anger is the seedbed of the Evil One, and he loves divisions, which can start as quite petty but grow into full-blown resentments. Jesus offers the more excellent way: to pray for those who persecute you and to be better than the pagans, who prefer only to love those who are easy to love. And by anticipating one another in showing kindness and gentleness to each other, husbands and wives must commit to not becoming the spouse who is difficult to love.

Question(s) / Prayer

Lord, help us to stamp out any pettiness and bickering in our marriage, which can become the cause of much deeper divisions. Help us to be self-aware of how we can bait the other into the divisions that the Evil One loves to sow. Grant us the graces of humility, forgiveness, and mildness, so that we bring joy and light for each other into our marriage.

EIGHTH SUNDAY IN ORDINARY TIME—YEAR A
GOSPEL: MATTHEW 6:24-34

Meditation

Anxiety is a part of life, but nowadays, it seems that more and more people find themselves overanxious about many things. Different sociological factors may contribute to this phenomenon, but it has spiritual dimensions too. Jesus offers us a healing word encouraging us to place all of our trust in him. So often, we act as if everything depends on us and as if Jesus only makes up for what we lack. But this is a recipe for overanxiety—and worse, it's not the way of the Lord. In fact, this attitude is born of an ancient heresy known as semi-Pelagianism. If we grasped that our mere existence is contingent upon God, we might find ourselves more detached from needless anxiety and freer to love and be loved. This is one of the reasons why faith-filled persons tend to live happier and fuller lives: They realize that their life is not their own and that they live and breathe under the watchful and loving gaze of the Father's providence. Within them there is a filial trust that the Father will provide for everything, and not just as a safety net or backup plan. When an individual lives this way, they will not want to serve mammon, referred to in the early portion of this gospel passage. They will only want to serve God, for they know to whom they owe their lives.

Question(s) / Prayer

Lord, teach us to trust in you and not ourselves. Put away all needless anxiety in our lives and in our marriage. May we perceive that you work through our material deficits in order to teach us to fully depend on your providential care. And may our real "anxiety" be an urgency to grow in the things that matter most to you.

NINTH SUNDAY IN ORDINARY TIME—YEAR A

GOSPEL: MATTHEW 7:21-27

Meditation

The Lord issues a warning and a safeguard against the sin of presumption. In the first half of this passage, he admonishes all those who exhibit an external piety and religiosity but fail to obey God's commands. In essence, Jesus warns us that it is not enough to claim a Catholic identity or a self-assured attitude of "I'm a good person" without living up to the demands of the Gospel, which are often at odds with worldly values and attitudes. For instance, one can excuse oneself from Sunday Mass (without just cause) with self-assurances that "God understands," which essentially supplants God's authority with one's own. But to counter this, Jesus offers us a simple solution: listen and obey him! Being faithful to the Lord requires our submission to his reign over our lives—a reign marked by true charity and righteousness before the Father. No matter what personal circumstances may seemingly eclipse us, if we remain rooted in the Lord, we have nothing to fear. If we find our solidity in Christ (and not ourselves), he will uphold us in our every need.

Question(s) / Prayer

Father, help us both to avoid the sin of presumption and to take care to place our trust in you. We often feel tempted to abandon the path you set before us when we think that we know better than you. Convert our hearts to see that you are working out our salvation through the storms of life and that you never forsake those who place their trust in you. May we take great consolation in obeying you, even when that is difficult and/or inconvenient, fully believing that you are our rock.

TENTH SUNDAY IN ORDINARY TIME—YEAR A

GOSPEL: MATTHEW 9:9-13

Meditation

Today's Gospel is the autobiographical account of the calling of St. Matthew. Jesus' choice of a public sinner to be an Evangelist and Apostle was scandalous to the Jewish religious elite. They could not fathom the possibility of a holy man like Jesus fraternizing with those whom the elite considered to be moral degenerates. And yet Jesus maintains a love for all persons, even sinners. That is not to say that he didn't call sinners to conversion or to say that he got co-opted into the lives of sinners. However, Jesus was not afraid to engage lost sheep in order to bring them home. Jesus refused to let human categories define who was save-able and who was not. For the Lord, anyone who seeks conversion and a faith-filled friendship with him is his kind of disciple. Notice that Jesus is not tainted by his engagement with Matthew. Instead, Matthew is sanctified by Jesus' presence and call. This should give anyone who feels discouraged by their sinfulness confidence that Jesus can save them, if only they will consent.

Question(s) / Prayer

Do we recognize Jesus' call to conversion in our lives? Do we attempt to make Jesus "fit" into our lifestyles, or are we willing to fit into his way of life—adopting his attitudes, priorities, and perspective? Are we ready to truly follow the Lord, like St. Matthew, or are we impeded by so many trivial and unimportant concerns and priorities that block our path to conversion and faith?

ELEVENTH SUNDAY IN ORDINARY TIME—YEAR A

GOSPEL: MATTHEW 9:36–10:8

Meditation

This passage is replete with themes regarding the vocation to the priesthood and religious life. One may ask if it has any relevance for those living the vocation to marriage. The answer is a resounding "yes," since it is in families that the attitudes needed to cultivate potential vocations are fostered. Virtues like charity, generosity, self-sacrifice, chastity, humility, and obedience are all necessary for young men to consider the priesthood and young men and women to contemplate religious life. If married people see the value of celibacy and how it witnesses to life in the world to come (where there is no human marriage), children can appreciate how God may call someone to forego the natural right to marriage in favor of an objectively superior state of life: consecrated celibacy for the sake of the Kingdom. It is edifying to witness families that honor those who are priests and religious and tragic to witness parents who give no serious consideration to the value of the priesthood or religious life for their own children. If families don't treasure and value those who have given up everything to serve the Church, why would children think that it's a life worth pursuing?

Question(s) / Prayer

Do we foster a culture of vocations in our family where children are not only free to pursue priesthood and religious life, but encouraged to remain open to the possibility? Would we consider having a priest or religious in our family a blessing or an impediment to our mere human desire to have grandchildren? Do we speak well of priests and religious in our family, and do our children know our priests and those serving in the consecrated life?

TWELFTH SUNDAY IN ORDINARY TIME—YEAR A

GOSPEL: MATTHEW 10:26-33

Meditation

In very apocalyptic terms, Jesus assures his followers of a great day of reckoning, when every secret will be made manifest and when God's justice will reign supreme—every wrong in the world will be set right, and the friends of Jesus will enter into the Father's glory, while his enemies will be cast into eternal darkness. Jesus assures his followers that this ought to give them confidence, especially in the face of injustice, oppression, and some of the absurd circumstances life can bring (for which there is often no mere human solution). This assurance should engender a complete filial trust in the Lord, who will not allow his enemies to triumph in the end. It is a stark reminder that while in this life we live in the Lord's mercy, we will live under his justice in the next. That is among the many consolations of believers. We will rejoice in the Lord's justice, not because of vengeance—but because he will truly reign and be all in all.

Question(s) / Prayer

Lord, help us to accept the injustices, oppression, and absurd circumstances of life, for which there is often no mere human solution. Help us to accept that there is often no resolution to expect in this life, but only in the next. And may our hearts not become hardened with vengeance, but only rejoice that your will be done on earth as it is heaven. Finally, help us to set aright any injustice that we may have perpetrated by seeking forgiveness from those whom we have offended.

THIRTEENTH SUNDAY IN ORDINARY TIME—YEAR A

GOSPEL: MATTHEW 10:37-42

Meditation

Jesus can only rightfully place himself above love of mother, father, son, or daughter because Jesus is Lord. This statement must have been shocking for the Jews to hear, because in the alignment of the Ten Commandments, familial love comes second only to love of God. The Lord's hearers would have had to conclude that the only way that Jesus could make this claim is if in fact he was God himself. The Lord's words are still challenging today. Very often, faithful and devout Catholics are asked to choose between obeying God and "keeping peace" in the family in the way of accepting illicit relationships, marriages outside the Church, non-practicing family members, and siblings who are not qualified to serve as godparents for Baptism or sponsors for Confirmation. Somehow, it is the devout Catholic who is expected to succumb to human respect or to honor family members above God—putting the devout Catholic in very uncomfortable positions. And yet how heroic it is to see parents and siblings who are trying to be faithful to the Lord refuse to give in and give recognition to sinful situations, all the while attempting to maintain a modicum of civility.

Question(s) / Prayer

Do we falsely live by the credo "family first" when it ought to be "God first"? Do we presume that "God will understand" when caving to pressure to put family members before the Lord's commands? Do we rationalize, asserting that "God wouldn't want me to be at odds with my family members" when in fact his words in today's Gospel suggest the opposite? Are we afraid of being "too Catholic" for our relatives, who themselves are in great need of conversion? Is this a blind spot in the way in which we relate to our family?

FOURTEENTH SUNDAY IN ORDINARY TIME—YEAR A

GOSPEL: MATTHEW 11:25-30

Meditation

In these six verses, the Lord presents us with the proper dispositions needed to walk with him on the journey of life. First, the aspiring disciple must not conflate worldly wisdom with knowledge and understanding of the things of God. The "wise and learned" of this world are liable to fall into the delusion of thinking that just because they are "somebody" in the world's eyes, their worldly success translates into salvific glory. Second, the "little ones" in the eyes of the world can be predisposed to receiving the Kingdom because of their total dependency on the Lord and his providential care. The God-reliant and not the self-sufficient person knows of their own need. That is why it is particularly inspiring to see those who are very successful in the eyes of the world carry themselves with an air of humility before God, knowing that all is gift from him, and then using those gifts to advance his Kingdom. Third, the image of the yoke is very instructive, as it demonstrates how God cares for us. Jewish farmers at the time of Christ utilized a double-harness yolk that permitted two animals to walk side by side, increasing the efficiency of the plowing. The Father is the farmer, the Lord is one of the animals, and we are the other. God expects us to cooperate with him and walk in sync with him. There is no passivity permitted in the life of a disciple. God remains in charge (as the farmer) but he also provides the assistance we need to push forward (the other animal who walks alongside us).

Question(s) / Prayer

Father in heaven, help us to acknowledge our need before you. When we tend towards the delusion of self-sufficiency, remind us that we are just one heartbeat from eternity, where none of our worldly accomplishments will "earn" us salvation, which is a complete and free gift from you alone. In our acknowledgement of need, help us to see that we must be active and engaged cooperators in working out our salvation in accord with your grace and mercy. Inspire us to break free from passivity and indolence into a space of ardor and zeal for your Kingdom.

FIFTEENTH SUNDAY IN ORDINARY TIME—YEAR A

GOSPEL: MATTHEW 13:1-23

Meditation

The Parable of the Sower and the Seed might be more aptly named "The Parable of the Four Soils." After all, neither the sower (the Lord) nor the seed (the Word of God) is variable. Both are immutable. The only variable in the parable is the type of soil that the seed lands upon. The soils, which represent our dispositions of receptivity, vary not only from person to person but within a person as well. Hence, an individual believer may have different types of soils within them. Some soil is very fertile and rich and other soil is rocky and covered with brambles. The goal is to be rich soil in all dimensions of our lives, so that the seed can germinate within us and bear a harvest worthy of the sower. Unfortunately, the work required to generate rich and receptive soil is not always easy. It requires a thorough and honest examination of conscience—one that presumes nothing about one's standing before the Lord. It also requires a strong and persevering resolution of the will to conquer vice, root out character defects and deficits, and grow in virtue. Many persons are discouraged by this internal struggle and prefer the easy and lazy road of mediocrity and indifference. But the parable reminds us to reject this indolence and strive for perfection.

Question(s) / Prayer

Lord, help us along the road of sanctity. Give us the courage to make a thorough and honest examination of conscience—one that presumes nothing about our standing before the Lord. Give us a strong and persevering resolution of the will to conquer our vices, root out our character defects and deficits, and grow in virtue. May we not become discouraged by this internal struggle, opting for what is easy—laziness, mediocrity, and indifference. Help us to strive for perfection.

SIXTEENTH SUNDAY IN ORDINARY TIME—YEAR A

GOSPEL: MATTHEW 13:24-43

Meditation

The Parable of the Weeds in the Field opens up important but difficult truths about God's Kingdom: First, the wheat and the weeds coexist under God's watchful gaze. Being someone whom God considers to be like a fruitful wheat crop does not eliminate the presence of the weeds in one's life. In other words, following Jesus does not mean that one's troubles immediately go away or that one now lives in a perfect society. And notice that the landowner (the Lord), in the interest of not bringing harm to the wheat, does not order the removal of the weeds. Instead, the wheat will have to figure out a way to exist in a field where the weeds may be prevalent and still bear fruit!

Second, the harvest imagery is a reminder of the decisiveness of the end of the world and the judgement of God. The weeds and the wheat receive proportionate and appropriate treatment. Part of the Gospel (good news) is that the just will receive their reward and the evil will receive their punishment—that is great news! But to live in the field of the world as if God does not exist is a dangerous decision. To ignore the call to faith and friendship with Jesus, for whatever reason, can be disastrous. And perhaps one of the greatest spiritual mistakes people make is to convince themselves that the harvest will go well for them simply because they "feel good" about their lives, even if the manner of their life shows little to no regard for the commandments of the landowner.

Question(s) / Prayer

Lord, give us clarity and discernment to accept that while we might consider ourselves wheat, we are in fact weeds. Help us to be humble in accepting that we might not be the fruitful wheat crop you desire, but are in fact weeds in the field of your Kingdom. If we are self-satisfied, help us to weed out that flaw in our mindset. If we are ambivalent about the Church's teachings or commandments and invent all kinds of pithy excuses for our indifference, help us to weed out those excuses as well, so that we might be spiritually transformed into the fruitful wheat crop you favor and gather into your barn.

SEVENTEENTH SUNDAY IN ORDINARY TIME—YEAR A

GOSPEL: MATTHEW 13:44-52

Meditation

The image of the Kingdom as a treasure in a field or a pearl of great price teaches us how radical following the Lord is. Those who have grasped the meaning and value of the Kingdom "sell the farm" in order to possess it. In other words, everything else in the world seems to take on very small importance when compared to the inexhaustible riches of the Kingdom. Discovering the treasure or the pearl compels one to re-orient one's life completely. Priorities change, lifestyle choices change, worldviews change, and affections change. The incredulous around them often call persons who undergo this conversion or reversion (coming back to the Faith) "really Catholic" or more benignly "devout." But the person who has experienced this dramatic re-orientation often considers themselves free and fulfilled. They often lament their pasts but give thanks for the present, while remaining hopeful for the future—especially as they seek to make the Lord all in all. These small miracles are very pleasing to the Lord, for they are signs of his grace and correspond to the motivation behind his Passion and death.

Question(s) / Prayer

What are the obstacles that prevent us from "selling everything" in order to possess the Kingdom? What latent fears stifle our conversion or reversion? Are we open to the possibility that every hallmark of success or security that we have built up for ourselves is really a façade, when compared to the depth and richness of the Kingdom? Or do we prefer to bet on the spirit of the world for our salvation?

EIGHTEENTH SUNDAY IN ORDINARY TIME—YEAR A

GOSPEL: MATTHEW 14:13-21

Meditation

Today's Gospel highlights the disciples' attempt to solve a dilemma with mere human solutions. Feeling the limitations of their resources (five loaves and two fish), they fail to leave room for the miracle the Lord is about to execute. Notice, however, that the Lord does not reject what little they are able to scrounge up. He takes their freely given meager resources and transforms them into a miracle that foreshadows the Institution of the Eucharist. The Lord takes human lack and turns it into divine abundance. It is very easy to think that whenever we need something, we ourselves have to create the solution(s). The Lord teaches us that he does not need our success—our fidelity to his plan and trust in his providential care are all he asks. We can become fixated on mere human solutions when what is needed is a divine remedy. And notice that it is not simply a case of Christ making up for what the disciples lack. Jesus had foreknowledge of this very scenario and set it up to teach the disciples that he does not simply fill in the gaps when and where we exhaust our own resources. Instead, Jesus is the font of even the small resources we can produce, and he allows us to experience lack so that we learn to trust in him fully. Jesus is never a victim of circumstance. Rather, he is in total control always and everywhere.

Question(s) / Prayer

Lord, grant us the grace to trust in you fully. Even when we cannot see or understand your plan for our lives, teach us to be docile and receptive. Whenever we desire to stray and "do it our way," help us to return to you with open hands and hearts. Expand our horizon and give us a new perspective so that we can perceive all that you are working out through the circumstances of life that you permit us to experience. In this way, teach us to be poor in spirit—completely dependent on you.

NINETEENTH SUNDAY IN ORDINARY TIME—YEAR A

GOSPEL: MATTHEW 14:22-33

Meditation

There's a small detail in today's Gospel that many overlook: When Jesus invites Peter to walk on the water, Jesus does not take away the stormy conditions. Rather, the Lord invites Peter to keep his eyes firmly locked on him and assures Peter of his presence and care. There's a great lesson in this small detail. Jesus does not promise us calm waters and smooth sailing—a life without trials or sufferings. Many choose to abandon friendship with the Lord because they have erroneous expectations about what discipleship means. They think that as long as they are faithful, the Lord will remove the Cross—even if the Lord promises that one must take up one's Cross and follow him in order to be his follower. Experience shows that even if the Lord won't remove the Cross, he never removes his love, providential care, and nearness to those who seek him with sincerity of heart. The miracles of the walking on the water and the calming of the sea demonstrate the Lord's omnipotence to the Apostles. They adore the Lord in the aftermath of having been brought to the brink of death. This provides an excellent inspiration to examine our personal and collective faith. It is easy to claim faith in the Lord until it is tested, even if not severely. And when it is tested severely, we discover the depth—or the lack thereof—of the roots of our faith.

Question(s) / Prayer

Lord, grant us the faith and hope to believe with our minds and trust with our hearts. May we learn the science of the Cross and not lose our grounding in your providential care when the storms of life seem severe and overwhelming. May we take great solace in the weakness of Peter, whom you saved even in his preoccupations and worries. May we only truly worry about losing our friendship with you, for you have conquered the world.

TWENTIETH SUNDAY IN ORDINARY TIME
GOSPEL MATTHEW 15:21-28

Meditation

The cultural dynamics present in today's Gospel are key to understanding the passage's deeper meaning. First, Jesus is a foreigner in a foreign land. He visits the Phoenician cities of Tyre and Sidon, which will provide the setting for an incredible demonstration of faith by the heroic Canaanite woman. His mere presence in Tyre and Sidon is a sign of Jesus' desire for the salvation of Jew and Gentile alike. This would have been shocking to the intended audience of St. Matthew's Gospel—Jewish communities who were potential converts to the Faith. Recall that the Jews believed that they had a monopoly on salvation, as God's Chosen People. Jesus is teaching his followers the opposite. Faith in him, not one's tribal or ethnic lineage, is the key to salvation. Second, the heroism of the Canaanite woman manifests immense audacity and courage. Imagine what it must have taken for a foreign woman in antiquity to address a nascent rabbi with a large following. She is undeterred by the social conventions of the time and presses forward with persevering prayer, akin to a beggar in desperate need. Jesus' seemingly harsh response is well calculated to draw out the woman's latent faith. And what he intended is precisely what transpires. Hence, there are two foreigners (the Lord and the Canaanite woman) in a foreign land engaged in the business of faith and salvation. We ought to marvel at the circumstances Jesus put together in order to teach us so many magnificent lessons.

Question(s) / Prayer

Lord, help us to appreciate contexts and backgrounds foreign to our own experience. Whenever we are tempted to think of the path to salvation as a private, monolithic road, help us to see that you provide multiple paths within the bounds of the salvific truths of the Faith to make our way home to the Father. Whenever we tend to think that the only way to heaven is the way we experience Catholicism, help us to see that there is a rich diversity within our massive family of faith, unbounded by our particular cultural milieu. May this truly "catholic" (universal) worldview help us to break free of the pervading tribalism of the day so that we can embrace as many believers as we can through the lens of our vocation.

TWENTY-FIRST SUNDAY IN ORDINARY TIME—YEAR A

GOSPEL: MATTHEW 16:13-20

Meditation

There are two answers to the question Jesus puts to the disciples in today's Gospel: "Who do you say that I am?" (Mt 16:15). First, Peter's confession of faith renders the objective answer—Jesus is the Christ! Its objective truth is confirmed by the Lord's statement that Peter's answer was given to him by the Father and not by "flesh and blood" (Mt 16:17). In other words, in a moment of infused knowledge, the Father grants Peter true insight into Jesus' true identity for the benefit of the others. Peter's answer isn't merely his opinion—he is speaking on behalf of the Father to give us the truth. Second, there is another dimension to the answer—the subjective dimension. In other words, each individual follower or would-be follower of Jesus needs to align the objective answer given by Peter with the subjective answer to the question, "Who is Jesus for me?" Problems arise when we exalt the subjective answer over the objective answer, thus creating a Jesus that caters to subjective desires and needs. The challenge of discipleship is to accept the objective answer and to align one's life (subjectively) with it.

Question(s) / Prayer

Lord, help us to align our subjective perceptions with the objective truth that Peter gives us in today's Gospel. May we trust that this re-orientation of our lives will provide the interior freedom that we all desire, knowing that we are not our own god, but your servants in faith, hope, and love. Help us to place you, and not our own egos, at the center of our lives and our marriage. May we become resolute in doing your will and not merely our own. And may we be eager to place our resources at your feet so that we can join Peter in acknowledging that you are truly the Son of God.

TWENTY-SECOND SUNDAY IN ORDINARY TIME—YEAR A

GOSPEL: MATTHEW 16:21-27

Meditation

Jesus admonishes St. Peter with very strong words: "Get behind me, Satan!" (Mt 16:23). Some have theorized that Peter's wish that the Lord might not fulfill his mission on the Cross ("God forbid, Lord!" (Mt 16:22)) reminded Jesus of Satan's forty days of temptations in the wilderness prior to the Lord beginning his public ministry. Just as Jesus reacted virulently to the Evil One's attacks, so was he moved in a similar way to scold Peter for Peter's worldly approach to Jesus' life, ministry, and mission. The Lord then goes on to connect the Cross with discipleship, telling his disciples that they cannot be his true followers without embracing their share of his sufferings. Peter's attitude is still very pervasive today in a world that prefers the couch to the Cross. Couples who are trying to live out their vocations faithful to the Church's teachings can often find themselves "tempted" by family members, friends, and the pervading culture to take on a worldly approach when it comes to living out the Faith. For instance, a faithful couple can be discouraged or even mocked for having more children, securing a solid formation for the family in the Faith, or ensuring that the family gets to Mass every Sunday, even on vacation. These wayward voices, like Peter's, must be vigorously opposed, even simply in the couple's ignoring the temptations.

Question(s) / Prayer

Lord, help us to keep our gaze fixed on you and to listen for your voice alone. May we always discern and evaluate the other voices in the light of our commitment to remain faithful to you, invoking the graces of our marital sacrament. May we not be swayed by voices that do not honor you as God, and may we find the courage to resist those who tempt us to abandon the Cross.

TWENTY-THIRD SUNDAY IN ORDINARY TIME—YEAR A

GOSPEL: MATTHEW 18:15-20

Meditation

The practice of fraternal correction has long been abandoned by many segments of Christian communities of faith. They prefer to gossip and speak *about* a person, rather than speak *to* the person themselves. Some prefer not to "get involved" under the guise of "minding my own business" or for fear of causing tension or conflict that may arise. This gospel passage enumerates the different steps one ought to take in giving and receiving fraternal correction, but all of these assume a few important values: First, we have an obligation to one another to speak up when sin is involved. To simply allow others to persist in their sin without any warning or correction would be tantamount to a doctor neglecting to tell a patient that they are very sick for fear that the patient may not like the news. Second, we need to put aside the human desire for respect or "being liked" when souls are at stake. It's much easier to "go along to get along" rather than address another person in love. Third, we need to be open to receiving fraternal correction. In order to be a part of a community of faith, we need to practice humility, docility, and trust that others have our true best interests at heart. It is only the arrogant and self-assured who have no bandwidth to receive fraternal correction. This is as serious a cancer as any other malaise in friendships, among family members, or in a marriage.

Question(s) / Prayer

Lord, grant us the discernment to be courageous in practicing fraternal correction. And make us so humble and meek of heart as to receive it whenever we sin. Grant us the freedom to invite correction from others so that we may strive for the path of perfection through the narrow gate. Help us to break from our spiritual laziness of silence for fear of disturbing what is an illusory peace. May we always remember that where you are not present, true peace cannot reign.

TWENTY-FOURTH SUNDAY IN ORDINARY TIME—YEAR A

GOSPEL: MATTHEW 18:21-35

Meditation

Mercy is one the key pillars of the Catholic moral tradition. Mercy is the capacity to reach beyond the line of strict justice between disputing parties and to enter into the paradigm of the other so as to find a path of moderation and forbearance that allows the two sides to reconcile and press forward. Mercy is never opposed to justice but tempers it and remains in dynamic tension with it. Moreover, it is divine mercy that instructs and gives shape to human mercy, which alone is insufficient. Mercy is so essential to the Christian life that it is referred to in both the Our Father ("Forgive us our debts" (Mt 6:12)) and the Beatitudes ("Blessed are the merciful" (Mt 5:7)). In spite of its challenging message, Christian mercy is not Pollyannaish. The Lord was well aware that forgiveness and mercy can be quite complicated, especially when one cannot reconcile with another person because one of the parties to the dispute might be dangerous or incarcerated or unreachable or deceased. Hence, the Lord says that, at minimum, the disciple must forgive "from his heart" in order to meet the standard Jesus sets for his followers. Marriage requires that spouses seek and grant mercy readily and consistently. Many marriages corrode under the rust of unforgiveness and/or a lack of awareness that one has offended the other. Humility, patience, and strong bias in favor of marital flourishing are crucial to a fruitful marriage in the Lord.

Question(s) / Prayer

Lord, help our marriage to be a place where mercy is freely given and sought. If we are easily offended as a result of our own woundedness, help us to offer that Cross for the other. If we easily offend, grant us the grace of mildness and graciousness that exudes the gentleness every spouse should expect from the other. May we be quick to ask for forgiveness and even quicker to grant it, always acting in favor of preserving and developing our marital love.

TWENTY-FIFTH SUNDAY IN ORDINARY TIME—YEAR A

GOSPEL: MATTHEW 20:1-16A

Meditation

While today's gospel passage is not intended to provide an example for a wage structure that could be taught in business school, it does give an insight into God's economy of salvation. The crux of this message is the reaction of the laborers who complain to the landowner for having paid the latecomers to the vineyard the same wage as themselves, who "bore the day's burden and the heat" (Mt 20:12). What the complaining workers fail to see is what a privilege it is to have been in the employ of the landowner for so long a time and to have been given the immense responsibility of cultivating the vineyard. They also fail to realize that their long and dedicated work was itself a gift and not a burden. What is more burdensome is not having been in the employ of the landowner—a description of the latecomers, who were idle. The Gospel challenges those who have been faithful to the Lord for many years to consider the immense blessings associated with this relationship. To see that faithfulness as a burden is a sign that the heart has yet to be converted to the Lord, for in that case one's true desire is to be apart from him and idle, at least spiritually speaking. To have lived in God's graces for many years is superior to not having been in friendship with him. It is distance from the Lord that is the true "day's burden and the heat."

Question(s) / Prayer

How do we view our friendship with the Lord—as a burden or limit on "our true selves," or as the path to authentic and genuine freedom that only he can provide? Do we envy the spiritually idle? Would we prefer to be listless and wandering? Or are we immensely grateful for the Lord's invitation to be his friend in the economy of salvation?

TWENTY-SIXTH SUNDAY IN ORDINARY TIME—YEAR A
GOSPEL: MATTHEW 21:28-32

Meditation

Today's gospel passage could be summed up with the cliché "Actions speak louder than words." Jesus' words to the chief priests and elders of the people would have been shocking not only to them but to the average man and woman hearing his words. After all, ordinary persons considered the chief priests and the elders to be assured of salvation because of their status as religious elites. But Jesus is not interested in their status or titles. Instead, he places a higher value on those who repent and experience conversion through faith in him. To the elites, Jesus was an upstart rogue rabbi, who was not part of their clique. They assumed that his lowly social status (compared to theirs) disqualified him from the inside track to salvation that they believed they held. On a deeper level, we can infer from the parable that while the son who actually did the father's will was more pleasing, the ideal son is the one who does both: He says he will obey and actually obeys. The challenge of obeying God is not simply complying with the commandments. At its deepest level, obedience entails wanting to obey the commandments because obedience is seen as a form of freedom and the path of love. It's one thing to do what one is told, begrudgingly. It's another thing to want to do what one is told.

Question(s) / Prayer

Lord, help us to do your will, to want to do your will, and to love your will. May we begin to see that obedience demands much more than mere compliance—that it means sharing in the mind and will of the lawgiver. Trusting that the Father's will is always worthy of our love, may we find interior freedom in our obedience, in spite of the sacrifices it may demand of us. May we take solace in the clear conscience that comes from genuine obedience, and may we teach our children that obedience is far superior to mere compliance, so that they interiorize the motivations for obedience and understand why it pleases God.

TWENTY-SEVENTH SUNDAY IN ORDINARY TIME—YEAR A

GOSPEL: MATTHEW 21:33-43

Meditation

Jesus' words in today's Gospel are an indictment of the Jewish chief priests and elders of the people. His words must have stung his hearers to the heart and convicted them of having squandered their opportunity to obtain fruit for God's Kingdom. Instead, the tenants in the parable (the chief priests and elders of the people) had become aggressive persecutors of those (the prophets) sent by the landowner (the Father), up to and including the murder of the landowner's son (Jesus). And in spite of Jesus addressing this parable directly to the Jewish chief priests and elders of the people, there's a lesson in the parable for all of us. We, too, run the risk of squandering our tenancy. We have been given so much and yet may end up having little to show for it when we face judgement. For instance, consider how lackadaisical our participation in the sacraments can be. Rank ambivalence pervades many sectors of the Church. And worse—we can also find ourselves unjustly persecuting those within the Church who are stalwarts of the Faith, those who preach the often difficult but true meaning of the Gospel. Bishops receive dozens of letters annually complaining about priests and religious who preach the Faith with authenticity and are rejected by their flocks for that very reason. Family members are at odds with those within their ranks whom they consider to be "too Catholic" because they do not compromise on principles to preserve an illusory "peace" or to just "get along" so that the erring can persist in their sins.

Question(s) / Prayer

What kind of accounting will we render unto the Lord for all the good he has done for us? Are we any better than the tenants in the parable? Are we open to being led by shepherds who lead us to Christ? Or do we prefer false shepherds who tell us simply what we want to hear to stroke our fragile egos? Do we realize that Jesus' words stung his hearers to the heart, and are we prepared to receive the same from good shepherds?

TWENTY-EIGHTH SUNDAY IN ORDINARY TIME—YEAR A

GOSPEL: MATTHEW 22:1-14

Meditation

The wrathful king in today's gospel passage offers us an insight into the urgency Jesus was attempting to impress upon his followers regarding the need to heed the invitation to and prepare for the wedding banquet (representative of heaven). In the first instance, invitees either ignore the invitation or make paltry excuses for non-participation. In the second case, the king does not take well the rejection of the emissaries he sends out for guests to the banquet (he burns the cities of those who do not accept the emissaries). In the third instance, those who accept the invitation but are unprepared (the guest not properly attired in a wedding garment) meet a sorry fate. There are many parables in the New Testament that communicate the consequences for rejecting and/or being unprepared for heaven. The hubris of the modern age is the assumption that everyone who dies goes to "a better place" in an attempt to console those who remain behind. The parable sends a diametrically opposed message. Presumption is a very dangerous attitude and sin. It fails to properly engage the eternal realities that await every human person in an attempt to avoid the conversion that Jesus demands of his followers. Presumption gives one permission to ignore, refuse, reject, and neglect the preparedness necessary for admission into heaven. This parable ought to compel us to consider where we stand before the Lord—from his perspective (not our own).

Question(s) / Prayer

Lord, help me never to presume my salvation or the salvation of anyone else. Whenever I am lackadaisical in my moral life or indifferent to conversion, help me to recall your stern warning in this parable. Whenever I conflate worldly comfort and success with the key to meriting eternal life, grant me a supernatural outlook that is honest and forthright before you. May I learn that the more quickly I admit my need for conversion, the closer I am to seeing your face. And may I gaze upon your blessed face for eternity with the saints.

TWENTY-NINTH SUNDAY IN ORDINARY TIME—YEAR A

GOSPEL: MATTHEW 22:15-21

Meditation

Jesus' words in today's Gospel give us guidance regarding Christian engagement with the world. The believer is not to become isolationist or insular. Rather, the believer is to fully engage in the affairs of the world, imbuing it with the spirit of the Gospel. This requires the believer to be conversant in the spirit of the Gospel and the Christian moral tradition so that these may inform and direct worldly affairs. The spiritual danger for believers is when the opposite occurs—when the spirit of the world, not the Gospel, becomes the operating principle. If the believer is not evangelizing the world, it will not be long before the spirit of the world guides their thinking and reshapes their priorities. And while it is tempting to disengage from the world and retreat into a "safer" mode of existence, this ethos is not consistent with the Gospel mandate to convert the world to the Lord. Hence, believers live in a world of dynamic tension: They must live in the world but not be co-opted by its spirit. This engagement with the world requires careful discernment to take what is good in the world and promote it, while critiquing worldly attitudes and reshaping them in line with the spirit of the Gospel. When believers excel in the professions, in the academy, and in civic life, they advance the cause of Christ for God's greater glory and the salvation of souls.

Question(s) / Prayer

How do we navigate the dynamic tension of living in the world but not being co-opted by its spirit? Are we entirely too worldly in our outlook? Do we tend to give Caesar his due to the neglect of the priority Christ ought to have? Or are we conversant in the spirit of the Gospel and the Christian moral tradition so that they inform and direct our engagement with the secular world?

THIRTIETH SUNDAY IN ORDINARY TIME—YEAR A

GOSPEL: MATTHEW 22:34-40

Meditation

The hierarchy of love that Jesus lays out in today's gospel passage has serious implications for married life. Notice that Jesus places God above all (yes, even above one's spouse and children), then oneself (in an ordinate way), and then others. While it may be counterintuitive to love oneself (in an ordinate way) before others, the logic is clear: It is necessary to take care of oneself so that one may become a gift to others. The purpose of this ordinate self-love is not selfish. Rather, it is motivated by a desire to save one's soul (out of love for God) and to bring others along. This hierarchy of loves is tested in any number of scenarios. For instance, a couple's adult child may reject their Catholic upbringing and marry outside the Church. Here, loving God above all others may require parents to abstain from participating or acknowledging the marriage, since it is not a marriage in the eyes of God. In another case, a young couple may need to select godparents from among their friends because the couple's siblings are not practicing Catholics. In yet other cases, one spouse may have to challenge the other spouse to spend more time with the family, instead of devoting so much time to a parish ministry. Love has to be ordered and proportionate in a way that respects the hierarchy of loves that Jesus describes.

Question(s) / Prayer

Lord, when we are tested to place ourselves or others before you, remind us that the first and greatest commandment is to love you with all of our heart, soul, mind, and strength. When we crave human respect or acceptance, help us not to give in to preferring those lesser goods to remaining faithful to you. And grant us the consolation of your Holy Spirit, who is our advocate and guide.

THIRTY-FIRST SUNDAY IN ORDINARY TIME—YEAR A

GOSPEL: MATTHEW 23:1-12

Meditation

In his critique of the scribes and Pharisees, Jesus uses three instances of hyperbole to point to the source of all teaching, fatherhood, and lordship: the Father. These expressions are not meant to be taken literally. Instead, they make the greater point that authority must be exercised in the name of service and that credible leaders always practice what they preach. The scribes and Pharisees had become notorious for creating layers of customary requirements that were burdensome for the Jews to practice. They had created a barrier between God and his Chosen People. And the religious leaders themselves had become accustomed to using their position to garner reputation and prestige. All of these things were inimical to the Lord's vision for religious practice. And as he established the Church and its leadership, he made it abundantly clear how he wanted authority exercised in his name. This has serious implications at all levels of the Church, especially in the home—the domestic church. Here, the faith itself and the spirit of the Gospel are passed down to children and future descendants. An ethos of humble, self-sacrificial service ought to pervade the culture of the family. An ethos of subordinating self-assertion to the greater needs and priorities of the family helps to cultivate the values Jesus esteems.

Question(s) / Prayer

How would we describe the culture of our marriage and family? Are its hallmarks humble and self-sacrificing service? Do we create an environment where subordinating individual preferences to the needs of the family comes naturally? Do we feel the liberating "weight" of passing down the faith and the spirit of the Gospel to our children and grandchildren? Do we impress upon them the need to pass along the torch of the Faith to successive generations?

THIRTY-SECOND SUNDAY IN ORDINARY TIME—YEAR A

GOSPEL: MATTHEW 25:1-13

Meditation

Some readers of today's Gospel may take exception to the unwillingness of the wise virgins to share their oil with the foolish ones. They may find it offensive that the only characteristic that we are told that separates the wise from the foolish virgins is their preparedness for the moment of the bridegroom's return. The decisiveness of the bridegroom's return (symbolic of the second coming of Christ to judge the living and the dead) points to a stark reality: We will all be judged individually. We will be judged neither as couples nor as families. Every individual is responsible for their own particular judgement at death. If we have a spouse or children or other loved ones who are not practicing the Faith, we may be judged in part on whether or not we made a sincere effort to help them return to the sacraments, but in the end—every man, woman, and child is responsible for their own outcome before Jesus. This should cause alarm in each of us if we are not making a sincere effort to help those who remain far from Jesus to return to him. None of us wants to hear those condemnatory words of the Lord when we meet him: "I never knew you" (Mt 7:23).

Question(s) / Prayer

Do we take the Lord's words seriously? If the parable resonates with us, what are we doing to warn our loved ones about the urgency of repentance even as we work out our own conversion? Do we love our loved ones enough to speak up? Or are we so paralyzed by our desire for human respect and "peace" in the family that we don't to speak up?

THIRTY-THIRD SUNDAY IN ORDINARY TIME—YEAR A

GOSPEL: MATTHEW 25:14-30

Meditation

The Gospel relates how the master of the servants went away for a long time. This small detail implies a spiritual danger for anyone in the employ of the master: the assumption that they have more time, or perhaps an indefinite amount of time, to make good on the investment entrusted to them. This can lead to boredom with spiritual matters (*acedia*), lukewarmness, and outright neglect. It's human nature to procrastinate when we perceive that requirements are not pressing. We can deceive ourselves into thinking that we'll make spiritual progress … eventually. Herein lies the warning of the parable: There is no indication when the master will return, and when he does—the master is very demanding. In fact, he calls the servant who produces nothing wicked and lazy! We might readily accept the criticism of laziness, but wickedness? To make matters worse for the servant who produces nothing, he knew that the master was demanding and yet did nothing about it. Citing the increasing number of inactive Catholics in the world today, we should all take heed not to fall into the same pitfall. That's not to say that active Catholics are already saints, but it is to say that it is far better to try to make good on the master's investment than not to attempt anything at all.

Question(s) / Prayer

Lord, help us to cooperate with your grace and be industrious in the business of the Kingdom. May we guard against *acedia*, lukewarmness, and spiritual neglect. Help us to avoid the spirit of presumption of our salvation and leverage all of our resources in favor of demonstrating our desire for heavenly glory on your terms and not merely our own.

The meditation for the Thirty-Fourth Sunday of Ordinary Time (Solemnity of Christ the King) is found below in the section "Solemnities and Feast Days of the Lord in Ordinary Time."

SUNDAYS IN ORDINARY TIME— YEAR B

SECOND SUNDAY IN ORDINARY TIME—YEAR B

GOSPEL: JOHN 1:35-42

Meditation

St. John records the decisive moment in his life when he first encountered the Lord. Jesus answers the deepest longing in the human heart—the desire for communion with God. He himself knows that he is the answer to the question that he asks John and the other disciple of John the Baptist: "What are you looking for?" The answer to their "what" is really a "who." This reveals the depth of Jesus' invitation to encounter him on the most profound level of human existence. Note that the disciples do not question Jesus about his doctrine. They simply want to abide with him where he dwells. And John vividly records that, at Jesus' invitation, they stayed with him that very day. And he says all this happened at four in the afternoon—an unusual hour to recall. Jewish time was often demarcated by multiples of three—"the third hour" (9:00 a.m.), "the sixth hour" (noon), "the ninth hour" (3:00 p.m.), and so forth. Hence, the recalling of four o'clock signifies that the Lord broke into these disciples' world in such a unique and atypical manner that it made a lasting impression on them and changed the trajectory of their lives forever.

Question(s) / Prayer

Have we experienced that breakthrough moment—that four o'clock hour in our marriage—when we decided to place our marriage completely in the Lord's hands, that decisive moment that forever changed the way we viewed each other *vis à vis* our salvation? Do we desire to take rest and solace in the Lord's embrace of friendship in such a way that we experience complete freedom to love and be loved? Do we want to abide in the Lord—to stay with him—in such a way the petty arguments or conflicts we have tend to shrink to the insignificant issues they usually are? Do we understand that truly abiding in the Lord gives us a new horizon and perspective regarding what truly matters in this life as it pertains to our destiny for heaven?

THIRD SUNDAY IN ORDINARY TIME—YEAR B

GOSPEL: MARK 1:14-20

Meditation

The central message of the preaching of Jesus is contained in today's Gospel: "Repent, and believe in the Gospel" (Mk 1:15). Repentance is not merely moral conversion. Rather, repentance entails a re-prioritization of one's life. It ranges from the dramatic to the subtle re-orientation of one's life to Christ. Moral conversion flows from this fundamental refocusing. Moral conversion is usually a sign of repentance, but the roots of repentance should run much deeper. This is precisely the re-prioritization that took place in the lives of the Apostles, also featured in today's Gospel. They left their former way of life and embarked on a profoundly new life in Christ. This repentance has to happen time and again in marriage. With so many seemingly important things (most are illusory, if we are honest) pulling at us and vying for our attention, we are in constant need to re-prioritize a life in Christ. This is marked by a more intentional discipleship rooted in serious prayer, complete participation in the sacraments, study of the Faith, and growth in virtue. It requires dying to the old self and beginning anew in Christ. In this model, Christ is no longer once of many voices we merely consume, like a favorite podcast or YouTube channel. Rather, he becomes the central protagonist in our lives, so that it is no longer the "I" who lives, but Christ who lives in me. Attempting to start with moral conversion, instead of a fundamental re-orientation of one's life to Christ, is usually short-lived. Hence, repentance rooted in faith in the Lord is the all-important priority.

Question(s) / Prayer

Where are the areas of our married life that still require genuine repentance? Do we assume that moral conversion is the starting point, or do we fully grasp the depth of authentic repentance—one that is rooted in faith and friendship with the Lord? Are we prepared to make those necessary re-prioritizations and re-orientations, so that Christ truly reigns in our hearts? What are concrete ways in which this faith-based repentance can start to take shape in our marriage?

FOURTH SUNDAY IN ORDINARY TIME—YEAR B

GOSPEL: MARK 1:21-28

Meditation

Those observing both the exorcisms and physical healings performed by Jesus are spellbound by his authority over the natural and supernatural worlds. Furthermore, the quality of his teaching style was compelling and markedly different from that employed by Judaism's official teachers. In these early verses of his Gospel, St. Mark is establishing the complete and total authority of Jesus as Lord of heaven and earth. Even the demons Jesus exorcizes know his identity and realize his power over them! This leaves no doubt that Jesus' dominion knows no bounds. In spite of this power, he rules with charity and never imposes himself on us. The human person remains radically free to accept or reject his Kingdom.

Question(s) / Prayer

Does Jesus reign as sovereign Lord in our marriage? Do we truly believe that his authority has jurisdiction over our decisions as a couple? And do we understand that Jesus' authority is not one of brute power or coercion? Instead, do we embrace his invitation to put the sweet yoke of his love upon our shoulders to help us carry the burdens of life? Are there still areas of our marriage where he does not reign supreme (commitment to prayer, being open to life in our marital relations, raising the children to be practicing Catholics)? What are we prepared to do to become his loyal subjects and even better—his friends?

FIFTH SUNDAY IN ORDINARY TIME—YEAR B

GOSPEL: MARK 1:29-39

Meditation

Twice in today's gospel passage, St. Mark indicates that the Lord "drove out demons" (Mk 1:33, 39). Across the four Gospels, Jesus performs a total of thirty-seven healings. Four of these (or ten percent) were definitive exorcisms. These do not include all the unrecorded exorcisms that Mark refers to in today's Gospel. These cannot be ignored, even if our popular culture relegates the presence and power of demons to the horror film genre or paranormal activity entertainment niche. In a materialist culture that dismisses the non-empirical as mythical, we can easily overlook the simple fact that while we are so enamored by the visible world around us, we often miss the invisible world, which is perhaps far more interesting. Even our Creed expresses God's dominion over all creation—the visible and invisible. Very few of us pay any attention to the snares of the Devil we acknowledge in the prayer to St. Michael the Archangel. And because we dismiss these realities as fictional, we also lose our sense of sin and of the spiritual combat being waged in and around us for souls. And yet, citing the high divorce rate in the West (with over half of marriages failing), can we not say that the world of the demons is real, even if their expulsion does not require a full-blown exorcism?

Question(s) / Prayer

Is the frequent reception of the Sacrament of Penance (or Reconciliation) a staple of our marriage? Do we realize that most of the demons in our lives can be cast out and kept out by the power of the grace of this sacrament? Do we even acknowledge the presence and power of demonic spirits who prowl about the world seeking the ruin of souls? And has an implicit denial or neglect of these realities created an indifference to sin in our lives?

SIXTH SUNDAY IN ORDINARY TIME—YEAR B

GOSPEL: MARK 1:40-45

Meditation

There is an important lesson to be culled from Jesus' admonition to the leper to keep the leper's healing a secret: the value of discretion. In a world that perhaps overvalues transparency, and conditioned by the "tell-all" media frenzies that dominate the news cycles with lurid stories of the vulgar and obscene, we can often forget about the value of keeping tight lipped about matters regarding our marriage. Pay heed here that this is not a warning against reporting criminal and/or dangerous behavior, especially when it compromises children and the vulnerable. Instead, the discretion should center around gossiping about one's spouse, which often devalues the reputation of the allegedly offending spouse in the minds of others close to the couple (family and friends). Rather than gossiping, it is much more constructive to speak to someone who can give spiritual advice and counsel and who remains outside the network of family and friendship bonds related to the marriage. Gossip is poison, and one ought to be very, very careful with whom information is shared. Besides adultery itself, nothing can poison the trust inside a marriage more than this.

Question(s) / Prayer

Do I gossip about my spouse? Does my indiscretion erode the trust in our marriage? Do I remain disciplined in only discussing marital matters with someone who can truly assist me with prudent and godly advice and who remains far enough removed from my marriage and family that what I reveal about my spouse will not harm their reputation? Or am I too quick to speak without discretion in such a way that injures my spouse and with persons who should not be involved?

SEVENTH SUNDAY IN ORDINARY TIME—YEAR B

GOSPEL: MARK 2:1-12

Meditation

The unsung heroes of today's Gospel are the four men who broke through the roof of the house in which Jesus was teaching and lowered the paralytic, placing him before the Lord. They are to be commended for their tenacity, their trust in Jesus' power to heal, and their sheer love for this helpless invalid. We do not know if they were friends of the paralytic, but we do know that they were willing to do whatever it took to give him a chance for a miracle. In marriage, sometimes a spouse is a paralytic and sometimes a spouse is one of the four men who puts the other before the Lord for healing. Trusting in the Lord to overcome the paralysis that a couple might encounter in their marriage is crucial to growing in a deeper relationship of faith in the Lord. Doing whatever it takes to be there for the other and a willingness on the part of the person who needs help take the very tenacity of the four men and the humility of the paralytic. Jesus saw all of this at work in this dramatic scene, and he always desires to heal all marital wounds.

Question(s) / Prayer

Father in heaven, please help us to know what role we need to play in giving and receiving help. Grant us the graces we need to bring to fulfillment the good work you have begun in us by having the courage to admit we need one another's help and the corresponding courage and compassion to assist the one in need. When the burden becomes too heavy, may you reveal to us the helpers we need to be able to accomplish your will.

EIGHTH SUNDAY IN ORDINARY TIME—YEAR B

GOSPEL: MARK 2:18-22

Meditation

Today's Gospel makes mention of a question posed to Jesus by the Pharisees in a controversy regarding fasting. This should cause us to consider the power and meaning of fasting. Fasting is a form of mortification (from the Latin, *mors* or death). In one aspect, fasting is the deliberate choice to forgo a good (usually food or drink) as a way of disciplining one's will to gain self-mastery and offer the sacrifice as a spiritual gift to the Father for an intention. Fasting need not only involve food or drink. One may choose to fast from expressing an unsolicited opinion or having the last word. It's a choice to not give in to one's initial inclination to indulge the body or one's pride (in the case of feeling the need to express oneself when it is not asked for). Nor is fasting merely dieting. Fasting's object or goal is primarily spiritual, not physical. The discipline of fasting places us in solidarity with the person for whom we fast—joining in their suffering in some small way and moving us to act on their behalf.

Question(s) / Prayer

Do we fast for each other? While it may be easier to pray for one another, do we offer spiritual sacrifices to the Father for the other's intentions? Do we fast from speaking, when what is needed is an open ear and a solid shoulder to lean upon? Are we so self-indulgent that we fail to see the high value of dying to ourselves for the sake of the other? Does fasting for our spouse help us grow in deeper love for them, since we move beyond mere romantic love into the realm of spiritual connection through fasting?

NINTH SUNDAY IN ORDINARY TIME—YEAR B

GOSPEL: MARK 2:23–3:6

Meditation

The man with a withered hand becomes caught in a polemic between Jesus and the Jewish authorities. The Jews want to entrap Jesus by accusing him of violating Sabbath law by performing a good work (the curing of the man with a withered hand). Not only does Jesus see through their hypocrisy and snares—he is the one who actually cares about the man with the withered hand. For the Jewish elders, the man with the withered hand (who represents a sinner) is inconsequential. They have little regard for him as a person. Instead, they are determined to achieve their end (Jesus' demise) no matter the cost. Their spiritual blindness is so malicious that Jesus looks at them with "anger and grieved at their hardness of heart" (Mk 3:6). Only Jesus loves the man with the withered hand (i.e., the sinner) and restores him to his dignity and place in the community.

Question(s) / Prayer

What are our spiritual blind spots? Do we have the honesty and courage to identify and resolve them with the Lord's help? Can we help each other see those hindrances to our spiritual maturity as individuals and as a couple, in a charitable and kind way? Are we willing to confess our sins regularly to root out those elements which prevent us from living out our vocation in freedom?

TENTH SUNDAY IN ORDINARY TIME—YEAR B

GOSPEL: MARK 3:20-35

Meditation

It is often said that blood (family loyalty) is thicker than water (a reference to our common humanity). However, the Lord's radical claim in today's Gospel suggests the opposite—that the water of Baptism is thicker than blood (family loyalty). In other words, Jesus is less interested in natural kinship (family) and more interested in spiritual kinship (solidarity among the baptized). That is why he says that his true relatives are those who do the will of the Father. In the case of our Lady, she was both his natural mother and the one who best did the Father's will. This spiritual kinship often comes into play when young parents are unable to select any of their siblings to serve as godparents because none of the siblings are practicing Catholics who qualify for the role. Instead, more and more devout parents seek practicing Catholic friends over family. This can often lead to divisions and resentments within families, not unlike what Jesus experienced when his relatives thought him to be "out of his mind" (Mk. 3:21). Jesus does not like divisions within families, but he accepts that divisions will occur, especially when not all of the family members are faithful to him.

Question(s) / Prayer

Lord, grant us the courage to stand up for you as your brother and sister, whenever we are persecuted or disenfranchised by our natural families for practicing the Faith in fidelity. May we take great solace in the solidarity of friendship that we experience with our friends in the Faith, even if they are not our blood relatives. Help us to find words that will help draw our wayward family members back to the Faith so that they may be counted among those who are known to you as your brothers and sisters.

ELEVENTH SUNDAY IN ORDINARY TIME—YEAR B

GOSPEL: MARK 4:26-34

Meditation

Mustard seeds are remarkably tiny, considering how large mustard plants grow to be. And when ground into mustard paste, the seeds are quite tangy in flavor. This is an appropriate image for the budding disciple of the Lord. Smallness or littleness has never been an impediment to advancing the Gospel. Think of the relative anonymity of Nazareth at the time of the Annunciation. Consider that the Lord started with a very small group of Twelve Apostles, none of whom had organizational leadership resumes. Imagine how a humble fisherman like St. Peter rose from obscurity to having the most famous church in the world built atop his tomb. If the project of the apostolate is the Lord's, he will secure its growth and fruitfulness. In the same way, most marriages are lived in ordinary communities and by ordinary spouses. This does not mean that a marriage cannot achieve great things—a loving and abundant family, a powerful witness to chastity and fidelity in a world that has abandoned self-sacrifice; perseverance when the Cross comes a couple's way. All of these require the couple to have that tangy tenacity to be holy and deliberate and focused on their vocation to sanctity. The mustard seed is a wonderful image for the way the Lord works out his providential plan of salvation.

Question(s) / Prayer

Lord, grant us the confidence to trust that you desire to guide and grace our marriage in its smallness and relative obscurity. Although our marriage may be unknown to most, may those it touches find it a sign of your abundant love and mercy for us poor sinners. May we never tire of witnessing to the power your grace brings into our lives and how it sustains us. Grant us the courage to have that mustard-like tangy edge to boldly proclaim your mercy and the fullness of joy that only your peace brings.

TWELFTH SUNDAY IN ORDINARY TIME—YEAR B

GOSPEL: MARK 4:35-41

Meditation

In shock and awe at the Lord's command over the natural order, the disciples ask, "Who is this whom even wind and sea obey?" (Mk 4:41). The question is very revelatory. At once, we see that the disciples struggled to understand the Lord. They were not always quick to understand or believe that Jesus is Lord. They may have regarded him as quite holy and erudite, but not omnipotent. And fewer things could demonstrate one's omnipotence in front of fisherman more than the capacity to command two of most feared elements they knew—wind and sea. Even before the miracle, they ask a question many of us may ask whenever we perceive the Lord's presence to be distant: "Do you not care that we are perishing?" (Mk 4:38). In a way, the questions themselves teach us more than the answers do. They make the disciples of Jesus much more relatable. They demonstrate all the basic fear and wonder that any of us would have shown if we had been personally present at the events. And the Lord's manner is remarkable: Jesus is calm and authoritative. He shows none of the doubts and fears that the disciples have. He has full trust in the Father and invites us to have the same.

Question(s) / Prayer

The wind and sea obey Jesus. Do we?

THIRTEENTH SUNDAY IN ORDINARY TIME—YEAR B

GOSPEL: MARK 5:21-43

Meditation

"And they ridiculed him" (Mk 5:40). Estimating their own point of view as absolute, those who mock Jesus are about to get a massive dose of reality. Little do they realize that the Son of God is going to raise Jairus's daughter from the dead, shattering all human expectations and understanding of death and the Lord's power over it. Not only does this demonstrate the Lord's omnipotence, it also teaches us to expect the unexpected when we "explain" our plans or opinions to God in prayer. Jairus sought out Jesus precisely because he knew no human solution would suffice to save his daughter—a sign of great faith. Jairus was risking his reputation as a synagogue official, since Jesus was considered by many of the ruling religious elite to be a questionable person. Jairus's prayer of desperation is what the Lord desires when we pray. Whenever we pray from a posture of self-sufficiency, we risk praying to ourselves and not to him. The broken and desperate individual is the one who can accept whatever the Lord offers and accept his will in peace. And peace is exactly what the Lord brings to the scene—he expels those making a commotion, replacing noise with the silence of his love.

Question(s) / Prayer

Lord, teach us to pray like Jairus—desperate and needy. Help us to realize how foolish our self-sufficiency is. May we learn to expel all the noise in our lives so as to usher in your loving silence, which is life-giving. May we never "ridicule" you for your ways, which can often challenge us to even greater faith and trust.

FOURTEENTH SUNDAY IN ORDINARY TIME—YEAR B

GOSPEL: MARK 6:1-6

Meditation

"Is he not the carpenter, the son of Mary…?" (Mk 6:3) is a question raised by skeptics regarding Jesus' public ministry. The question is leveled as an insult, since carpenters were not regarded as high-status workers in Jesus' time. And yet the Lord was proud to be the son of a carpenter (St. Joseph) in spite of the saint's lowly stature in worldly terms. Joseph taught the Lord (in his humanity) the value of hard work and how to memorize the Psalms (which were commonly prayed while working). The Lord's familiarity with woodworking would reach its climax as he was fastened to the wood of the Cross on Good Friday. The Lord purposefully chose to place himself under the care of a man who is heralded for his virtue, not his career or worldly status. This is another way in which the Lord remains eminently accessible to the human race—all of the marks of his humble birth and upbringing and human family help all persons draw close to him and the Holy Family. This is the way of the Lord—not allowing mere human conventions to disqualify anyone from conversion and faith in him. Jesus does not intimidate or "outclass" anyone. He retains his dignity without lording it over those who are "less" in the eyes of the world, so long as they have faith in him and seek the Kingdom through repentance.

Question(s) / Prayer

Do we retain a certain air of inaccessibility that prevents us from spreading the Kingdom of the Lord? Are we too bound to human conventions that serve as obstacles to the works of mercy (corporal or spiritual)? Are we too afraid to engage those outside our comfort zone because we're afraid of what people will think if we reach out to them? Is this a true imitation of the Lord?

FIFTEENTH SUNDAY IN ORDINARY TIME—YEAR B

GOSPEL: MARK 6:7-13

Meditation

The Lord gives his disciples very specific instructions about how they are to conduct their ministry. These precise instructions are designed to help all followers of Jesus to avoid several pitfalls: First, the instruction to go out in pairs is designed to create a culture of accountability and support. Left to our own devices, individuals can fall into pride and/or discouragement when evaluating their effectiveness in the apostolate. A good partner will always keep the other person humble, grounded, and hopeful. Second, the instructions regarding food, clothing, and money are designed to teach the disciple dependency upon the Lord's providential care and detachment from material creature comforts, and to be a check against self-sufficiency. It's quite tempting to think that one can do one's best and God will do the rest. This semi-Pelagian mindset (a heresy condemned in the fifth century) asserts that God makes up the difference when and where our resources run out. Christ reminds us that from beginning to end, all is grace and all the good we do is a participation in God's goodness. By ourselves, we can do nothing, if we are honest. While the Lord's words were once directed to those whom he commissioned to preach the Gospel in a formal way, these dispositions apply to all vocations and are necessary guides for fruitfulness.

Question(s) / Prayer

Do we tend to think that the project of personal sanctity is best done alone? Do we see the value of the communal aspect of growth? Do we tend to overly privatize our faith journey, or are we open to the benefits that community life can offer? In our attempts to evangelize, are we too entirely self-sufficient, or do we beg the Lord for his essential help, which is the animator of any genuine effort?

SIXTEENTH SUNDAY IN ORDINARY TIME—YEAR B

GOSPEL: MARK 6:30-34

Meditation

In inviting his followers to come away by themselves and rest a while, Jesus teaches us a few important lessons: First, rest is part of the created order. God himself rested on the seventh day, to provide the pattern and example for our Sabbath. For us, rest is not just a physical need, but also answers the spiritual yearning to re-create. It is an opportunity to re-center ourselves on the Lord in worship, to reflect upon our lives and our relationships with him and with our loved ones, and to allow the mind and heart to heal from the chaos so prevalent in contemporary life. Rest allows us to be alone with the Lord and ourselves, calming the frenetic cacophony of modern busyness so that we can trace a life narrative (story) of where we came from, where we are, and where we are going. It is restorative and humanizing and predisposes us to receive the Lord's blessings and promptings as gift.

Question(s) / Prayer

Do we give in too easily to the rat race? Are we living in a constant state of exhaustion and spiritual fatigue because we fail to accept the Sabbath as gift? Are weekends simply given to too much activity, so that the concept of a Sunday (the Lord's Day) is not a priority? Are we unable to trace a life narrative because we work and live at a pace that makes it nearly impossible? What are we prepared to do to reclaim God's desire for us to come away and rest a while?

SEVENTEENTH SUNDAY IN ORDINARY TIME—YEAR B

GOSPEL: JOHN 6:1-15

Meditation

Today's Gospel highlights the disciples' attempt to solve a dilemma with mere human solutions. Feeling the limitations of their lack of resources, they fail to leave room for the imminent miracle the Lord is about to execute. Notice, however, that the Lord does not reject what little they are able to scrounge up. He takes their freely given meager resources and transforms them into a miracle that foreshadows the Institution of the Eucharist. The Lord takes human lack and turns it into divine abundance. It is very easy to think that whenever we need something, we ourselves have to create the solution(s). The Lord teaches us that he does not need our success—our fidelity to his plan and trust in his providential care are all he asks. Moreover, we can become fixated on mere human solutions, when what is needed is a divine remedy. At times, we forget that the human person is not just a biological organism. And so we attempt to "solve" problems by throwing material resources at them. It is so often the case that what the situation needs is prayer, fasting, and the cultivation of the interior lives of all whom we attempt to assist. Only the Lord can offer the full complement of solutions that we seek.

Question(s) / Prayer

Father, help us to lift up our gaze towards you. Whenever we are too humanistic in our approach, grant us the grace to be open to the divine solution that only you can provide. When we feel frustrated by our lack of resources or support, help us to recall that every blessing (material or spiritual) comes from you and that you will help us find our way. In prayerful discernment regarding difficult situations, aid us in our willingness to turn our concerns over to you and to experience the liberty of knowing that you will come to our assistance.

EIGHTEENTH SUNDAY IN ORDINARY TIME—YEAR B

GOSPEL: JOHN 6:24-35

Meditation

Jesus uses the feeding of the multitudes (which precedes this scene) as a foreshadowing of his establishment of the Sacrament of the Eucharist. In John's Gospel, chapter six is dedicated to the Eucharist (there is no mention of it at the Last Supper, even if that scene covers five chapters in John's Gospel). The Lord uses the experience of manna in the desert during the time of the Exodus as the interpretive lens through which the disciples can understand how he is about to give them the very source and summit of the Church's life. And yet the followers of Jesus see him as a mere "bread king" who feeds the multitudes on command and satisfies their bodily hunger. Jesus desires to do something much more—to give them the bread that always satisfies the soul, even in the face of bodily hunger. But to comprehend this work of the Father requires faith, which is not a suspension of reason, but its fulfilment. Faith knowledge does not contradict rational knowledge. Instead, it expands it and gives it the depth that only human persons and angels can begin to comprehend. As is so often the case, Jesus is expanding how his followers perceive him and revealing more of the richness of what he desires to give—his very body, blood, soul, and divinity in sacramental form.

Question(s) / Prayer

Do we take the Eucharist for granted? Do we see it as true communion with the Lord? Do we understand the relationship between our state of soul, the need for regular Confession, and our "worthiness" to receive this most precious gift? Like the Eucharist, which is broken and spent for others, do we pour out our lives for one another as a living sacrifice of praise to the Father?

NINETEENTH SUNDAY IN ORDINARY TIME—YEAR B

GOSPEL: JOHN 6:41-51

Meditation

Forms of the word "murmur" appear twice in today's Gospel. Jesus' teaching on the Eucharist is met with doubt and even rejection. The Lord set up the very manner in which he wanted to remain with us until the end of the age, as he would promise the Apostles at the Ascension. And the Eucharist, as the source and summit of the entire Christian life, is that precise gift that Jesus has bestowed upon the Church, the gift that sustains her and animates all of her charitable works and evangelization. The Eucharist inspires vocations to the priesthood and religious life and vivifies marriages to allow spouses to remain united in the Lord. Jesus admonishes his hearers to stop murmuring so that they can properly receive all that he wishes to give. And he can only command this attention because he is the Lord. To be fair to his original hearers, Jesus was making mighty claims that seemed almost outrageous to them. The individual prospective follower of the Lord must make a choice—to believe Jesus or not. And belief does not require the suspension of reason. Instead, faith fulfills and transcends reason's deepest yearnings.

Question(s) / Prayer

How Eucharistically-centered are we as individuals and as a couple? Do we tend to murmur about the reality of the Blessed Sacrament, perhaps doubting that we must be free of mortal sin in order to receive the Lord "worthily"? How often do we go to adoration of the Blessed Sacrament to place ourselves in the holy presence of God, literally, so that we may be counted among his friends? Do we take time to prepare for Mass by arriving early, and do we stay for a few moments after the final hymn so as to make a thanksgiving for the inestimable gift we have received? Or do we casually roll into Mass and leave as soon as we can?

TWENTIETH SUNDAY IN ORDINARY TIME—YEAR B

GOSPEL: JOHN 6:51-58

Meditation

In no uncertain terms, Jesus connects salvation to communion with his body and blood. He says that unless one eats the flesh of the Son of Man and drinks his blood, one does not have life within them. That is a very serious and dramatic claim! And it is one of the main motivations for daily communicants to remain faithful to that discipline—they want to have the life of Jesus coursing through their veins! And yet, how sad it is to see so many Catholics (practicing and non-practicing) approach the Eucharist with a casual and nonchalant attitude. It is easy to treat communion with the Lord like the consumption of any ordinary good, when in fact the Eucharist *is* Jesus himself! Many Catholics approach the Lord not properly disposed (i.e., in a state of mortal sin) and think very little of missing Mass on a regular basis (itself grave matter). The premium importance the Church places on the Eucharist has deep implications for a sacramental marriage. Many Catholics think that the foundation of their marriage is *their* love. That love can be quite fickle and, unfortunately, unfaithful and/or negligent. The true foundation of marital love is God's love for the couple and the self-sacrifice of Christ they are called to imitate. Hence, it takes five to get married: the Holy Trinity and the couple. A couple's love alone will fizzle and fade and evolve over time. The love of God is immutable—and the constancy a couple needs to stay together.

Question(s) / Prayer

When we encounter turbulence in our marriage and even deep crises, do we choose to remain in the marriage simply because of the other person, or out of love for God? Do we realize that if it is the former, the marriage will almost always fail and if it is the latter, the marriage has a chance? Do we understand that the rigors of marriage require a personal relationship with the Lord as its bedrock, so that we can become astute disciples in the school of self-sacrifice? Jesus is broken and spent in the Eucharist. Do we do the same in our marriage?

TWENTY-FIRST SUNDAY IN ORDINARY TIME—YEAR B

GOSPEL: JOHN 6:60-69

Meditation

For many of Jesus' original followers, his doctrine on the Eucharist was too much to accept. The Gospel relates how many of them returned to their former way of life and no longer followed the Lord. In a moment of utter decisiveness, the Lord puts the Apostles to the test and asks them if they too want to leave him. St. Peter, speaking for the group, famously reasserts their faith in Jesus' divinity and answers Jesus' question with his own: "To whom shall we go?" (Jn 6:68). There is no middle ground when it comes to following the Lord. Either one is "all in" or one is forced to live a compromised Catholicism, set on one's subjective terms and not the Lord's. This type of commitment makes many a modern person uncomfortable since it can appear to them to be "fanatical" or "radical" or "too Catholic." And yet the Eucharist demands this kind of response. In other words, there are two types of people in the world: those who believe in the Eucharist and those who don't. And if the Eucharist is the Lord, then every other aspect of one's life is contingent upon living in a way that corresponds to that reality. There is no middle ground.

Question(s) / Prayer

Are we comfortable with being considered "fanatical" or "radical" or "too Catholic," when in fact all we are doing is taking the Lord's words at face value and trying (by his grace) to follow him? Are we too beholden to worldly opinion or fashion to embrace the Lord's saving gift of his body, blood, soul, and divinity? Do we prefer to return to our former way of life and no longer follow the Lord on his terms?

TWENTY-SECOND SUNDAY IN ORDINARY TIME—YEAR B

GOSPEL: MARK 7:1-8,14-15,21-23

Meditation

Jesus openly criticizes the religious externalism of the Pharisees and scribes in today's Gospel. Over the centuries, Judaism had adopted many external practices that became more important than the internal attitudes and dispositions that should have been animating them. Jesus is not opposed to external practices per se, but he expects the observance of externals to come from an internal disposition of true piety, reverence, and love for the Father. When externals become ends in themselves, versus means to personal conversion, or when the observance of externals does not correspond to a life of holiness, something is askew. While the elders of the Jews were concerned with the poorly practice of externals that they believed defiled their coreligionists, Jesus' list of things that defile all begins with internal vices. In the Lord's view, it's not either the externals or the internals. Rather it's both the externals and the internals, lived in an integrated manner. Quoting the prophet Isaiah, Jesus warns his hearers that God is displeased with those who honor him with their lips but have hearts that are far from him.

Question(s) / Prayer

Where are there disconnects between our internals and externals? Do we practice what we preach? Do we claim to be Catholic but not practice the Faith according to the Church's teachings? Or do we practice the Faith by the book but lack charity, generosity, and the forbearance needed to cultivate interior virtue? Are we cognizant of the canon (list) of internal dispositions that Jesus says defile one from within, or have we made "peace" with some of these sins, so that they remain hindrances to our growth in sanctity?

TWENTY-THIRD SUNDAY IN ORDINARY TIME—YEAR B

GOSPEL: MARK 7:31-37

Meditation

Today's passage includes what modern Westerners may consider some unusual details regarding the healing of the deaf and mute man. Jesus seems to engage in unsanitary practices that invade personal space norms, which compels us to question what is at work in this healing. First, notice that Jesus' "technique" is quite earthy and tactile. The idea here is that Jesus enters fully into the human condition, sharing in all of its filth and unsavory dimensions—in all things but sin. The Lord does not keep a "safe" distance from those who need him. He draws very close to us—he is as near to us as our breath. Second, Jesus does not become contaminated by touching a man with a deformity. In the Judaism of the Lord's era, physically touching the sick made one ritually impure for worship in the Temple, and one would need to engage in all kinds of symbolic ritual purifications to re-enter God's holy presence. Here, we see the reverse: Jesus purifies the physical deformity of the deaf and mute man, and the Lord himself is not compromised. Third, Jesus heals personally. Notice that the Lord takes the deaf and mute man away by himself to engage him one on one. Jesus does not heal merely "in principle" or "theoretically" but personally and truly. He reaches into the core of the man (his soul) and restores his dignity (symbolized by good health). This regeneration of the deaf and mute man, who was once compromised by sin (symbolized by the deformities) is a metaphor for the healing in the Sacrament of Penance (Reconciliation).

Question(s) / Prayer

How often do we go to the Lord for the healing of our spiritual deafness and unwillingness to proclaim all the good he has done for us? Is the Sacrament of Penance a regular or rare experience for us? Do we tend to think of healing as merely psychological, addressed by counseling? Or do we see that true healing also involves spiritual restoration and moral conviction?

TWENTY-FOURTH SUNDAY IN ORDINARY TIME—YEAR B

GOSPEL: MARK 8:27-35

Meditation

Jesus admonishes St. Peter with very strong words: "Get behind me, Satan!" (Mk 8:33) Some have theorized that Peter's wish that the Lord might not fulfill his mission on the Cross reminded Jesus of Satan's forty days of temptations in the wilderness prior to the Lord beginning his public ministry. And just as Jesus reacted virulently to the Evil One's attacks, so too was he moved in a similar way to scold Peter for his worldly approach to Jesus' life, ministry, and mission. The Lord then goes on to connect the Cross with discipleship, declaring that one cannot be his true follower without embracing one's share of his sufferings. In a world that prefers the couch to the Cross, this attitude is still very pervasive today. Couples who are trying to live out their vocations faithful to the Church's teachings can often find themselves "tempted" by family members, friends, and the pervading culture to take on a worldly approach when it comes to living out the Faith. For instance, a faithful couple can be discouraged or even mocked for having more children, securing a solid formation for the family in the Faith, or ensuring that the family gets to Mass every Sunday, even on vacation. These wayward voices must be vigorously opposed, even simply in a couple's ignoring of the temptations. These voices must be recognized as thinking as human beings do and not like God.

Question(s) / Prayer

Lord, help us to keep our gaze fixed on you and to listen for your voice alone. May we always discern and evaluate the other voices per our commitment to remain faithful to you, invoking the graces of our sacrament. May we not be swayed by voices that do not honor you as God, and may we find the courage to resist those who tempt us to abandon the Cross.

TWENTY-FIFTH SUNDAY IN ORDINARY TIME—YEAR B

GOSPEL: MARK 9:30-37

Meditation

Jesus' words in today's Gospel form the basis for the idea of Christian servant-leadership, a very popular leadership theory even taught in secular institutions. Many non-Christians find this model very appealing, but there is a dimension of it that many of them ignore—Jesus' use of a child to help us understand the proper dispositions needed to carry out Christian servant-leadership. For the secular person, a servant-leader can still exercise absolute autonomy from God, a type of self-determination that employs a servant-minded altruism as a way of leading others. Meanwhile, the Christian who engages in Jesus' model of servant-leadership is first a leader who actively discerns God's will by being attentive and totally dependent on how the Lord wants to move others to success and—ultimately—to salvation. The true Christian servant-leader always maintains a posture of openness to being led by God's will. Hence, the true Christian servant-leader is first a listener. They attempt to communicate God's lordship among those being led. And this lordship dies to self and places the needs of the group ahead of any individual interests, imitating the Lord himself.

Question(s) / Prayer

Father in heaven, whenever we have to make decisions for our marriage and family, help us to begin by first listening to you. May we learn to lay our biases and/or preferences at your feet for your guidance. And may we extend this posture of listening and openness to all aspects of our lives, even those beyond the family. Like a child, may we learn to depend on your voice to know your will and not give its primacy a mere courteous nod that bears no real significance for how we decide the best course of action. Like Jesus, who was always in communion with you, help us to enter into that communion of love so that we may try to cooperate with your will.

TWENTY-SIXTH SUNDAY IN ORDINARY TIME—YEAR B

GOSPEL: MARK 9:38-43,45,47-48

Meditation

In the second part of the gospel passage, Jesus explains the sin of scandal—actions, words, or attitudes that lead others into sin. The "scandal" that Christians should avoid is derived from a Greek word that means obstacle or stumbling block. Here, "scandal" does not necessarily carry the popular meaning of the word, which entails shock or surprise at immoral behavior. A contemporary example may help distinguish the two meanings: Today, it is very common for unmarried couples to live together as if they were husband and wife. It is so commonplace that hardly a person thinks it odd or unusual, let alone immoral. So, in the popular sense of the word, cohabitation does not give scandal. But in the moral sense of the word, cohabitation is quite scandalous, since it leads others to believe that such behavior is not immoral (even if it is, hence the term "living in sin"). It can lead the young to believe that such behavior is normative, and even virtuous, when in truth, cohabitation is solemnized fornication. Jesus warns against scandal in very severe terms, and it is the duty of parents and the community to guard the purity of the young from attitudes and behaviors that ignore the moral law and lead others to do the same. This requires a refinement of conscience, commensurate with the teachings of the Lord.

Question(s) / Prayer

Do we recognize scandal in the moral sense of the term? Or do we give tacit endorsement to it? Are we prepared to speak up when others act scandalously and to explain to our children why such behavior is wrong? Or do we too easily surrender to the worldly immorality of the day, paying little to no regard to the disconnect between the Faith we claim to profess and the immorality we ignore or refuse to confront?

TWENTY-SEVENTH SUNDAY IN ORDINARY TIME—YEAR B

GOSPEL: MARK 10:2-16

Meditation

There is no more specific teaching that Jesus gives in the entire New Testament than that regarding divorce and remarriage. Jewish practice had permitted divorce due to the "hardness of heart" (Mk 10:5) that Jesus references in his reply to the Pharisees. In fulfilling this teaching and bringing it to perfection, the Lord directs us back to the original plan for marriage, established in the Book of Genesis in the persons of Adam and Eve. What Jesus is saying is that divorce is not merely immoral—it is impossible, since man must not separate what God has joined. Hence, the annulment process is not Catholic divorce. Rather, an annulment declares that at the time of the wedding, something was lacking in the consent of the couple that hampered them from establishing a covenant of marriage. A civil divorce, by contrast, states that a couple was married on a certain date and terminated the relationship at a later date. An annulment states that the couple was never married at all (there are no implications for the moral standing of the children). Until and unless Catholics who are civilly divorced are granted an annulment, they are bound by their marital promises. This respects the Lord's teaching on the indissolubility of the bond, which remains sacred. In a culture replete with divorce, this teaching is truly counter-cultural and a witness to what God has established through marriage.

Question(s) / Prayer

How do we reach out to those disaffected by divorce and remarriage? How do we accompany Catholics to and through the annulment process if they have regrettably married outside the Church and are therefore not married? Do we understand Christ's teaching on divorce and remarriage and communicate this to our children? Do we treasure the graces of the Sacrament of Marriage, so necessary for a marriage in Christ to thrive?

TWENTY-EIGHTH SUNDAY IN ORDINARY TIME—YEAR B

GOSPEL: MARK 10:17-30

Meditation

Notice that the rich young man in today's gospel passage remains nameless. This was a technique used by ancient writers to communicate that the rich young man could be understood as a representative of many a man, past and present. The fact that he went away sad on account of his many possessions must have been shocking to Jesus' hearers. After all, Jewish society, like many societies today, revered men who were young and rich. At the time of the Lord, men were the real power brokers of society. Women had few to no civil rights, so men held all the temporal power in society. And the rich were considered blessed by God, since they appeared to many to carry the many weighty responsibilities of life in the ancient world. The young were also envied because their vigor represented health and a path to the future. But while the rich young man excelled in many worldly categories, he was unable to perceive the greatest good he had ever encountered (the Lord!). Society and the Gospels have very different definitions for what constitutes success. This parable should cause its hearers and readers to consider carefully how Jesus defines "success" relative to more worldly definitions. Even today, an unwillingness to prioritize what matters to God causes the worldly to go away from Jesus in sadness.

Question(s) / Prayer

Lord, help us to peer deeply into how we measure our positioning for the ultimate happiness of possessing you. If possessing you is not our top priority because we are too attached to worldly benchmarks of success and the pride of life, fill us with your Holy Spirit so that we might re-evaluate everything in light of knowing and possessing you alone. May turning to you with our whole lives cause us joy, not sorrow. And unlike the rich young man, may we never lose you from our grasp.

TWENTY-NINTH SUNDAY IN ORDINARY TIME—YEAR B

GOSPEL: MARK 10:35-45

Meditation

Episodes such as the one depicted in today's Gospel remind us of the humanity of the Apostles. Not having fully grasped the Christian approach to leadership and service, they require the Lord's admonition and formation to correct their worldly attitudes. This scene also demonstrates the authenticity of the Gospels themselves, as they indicate that the Apostles were flawed heroes, still learning the way of the Lord Jesus. If the Gospels were mere propaganda, they would not include this less than flattering depiction of the Apostles' attitudes. This ought to give believers of every generation great consolation. The Lord did not pick these men because they were perfect or because they were quick to learn his way. In other words, they were not qualified to aspire to the lofty role they would play in the Church. Instead, Jesus himself is their credential—*he qualifies them*. And so it is with every believer. None of us is "worthy" on our own merits. But the Lord elevates us to a higher dignity not known to man before he came among us. The issue that remains for every disciple regards their willingness to be formed in the school of Jesus—to learn his attitudes, his viewpoint, his priorities, and his way of love.

Question(s) / Prayer

Lord, help us to learn! When we default to viewing the Gospel through political categories, help us to understand that you remain above mere human conventions. When we seek human solutions to problems that require a divine remedy, elevate our thoughts and hearts to seek you alone. When our horizon is limited by human possibilities, help us to trust that you can transcend even these by your grace.

THIRTIETH SUNDAY IN ORDINARY TIME—YEAR B

GOSPEL: MARK 10:46-52

Meditation

Bartimaeus has to overcome the hostility of those around him and their rebuke—telling him to be silent. Grace compels him to call out all the more: "Son of David, have pity on me!" (Mk 10:47). There are many voices in our lives that try to silence or dampen our zeal for Jesus. The voices can range from the family member or friend or colleague who scoffs at our faith to the voice of self-doubt that causes a wavering faith in the midst of suffering or difficulties. Grace is available to us to call out all the more to the Lord with confidence. May we never listen to all the voices that seek to dissuade us from communion with the only One who can save us. And when we come face to face with Jesus who asks us what we want him to do for us, may we have the right answer: "Master, I want to see!" (Mk 10:51). The sight that we ought to be asking for is not physical sight. Rather, it is the capacity to see with the eyes of the heart. In other words, it's the ability to perceive spiritual goods that makes us sensitive to the promptings of the Holy Spirit that move us into the worldview and perspective of the Lord. These are the eyes that assist us to choose true goods that orient us to the will of the Father. And these are the eyes that give us insight into the plight of others and foster compassion and understanding on our part.

Question(s) / Prayer

Lord, help me to cry out to you with the faith and determination of Bartimaeus. Help me to banish all doubt and to filter out those voices that are not from you. May my faith cause doubt in the naysayers and inspire them to seek you. Heal the eyes of our heart. Help us to have true vision to perceive all that you desire to enliven in us in your Holy Spirit. As we seek to see you, grace us with the courage to accompany others along the paths of righteousness and holiness so that they too may see!

THIRTY-FIRST SUNDAY IN ORDINARY TIME—YEAR B

GOSPEL: MARK 12:28B-34

Meditation

The hierarchy of love that Jesus lays out in today's gospel passage has serious implications for married life. Notice that Jesus places God above all (yes, even above one's spouse and children), and then oneself (in an ordinate way), and then others. While it may be counterintuitive to love oneself (in an ordinate way) before others, the logic is clear: It is necessary to take care of oneself so that one can become a gift to others. The purpose of this ordinate self-love is not selfish. Rather, it is motivated by a desire to save one's soul (out of love for God) and to bring others along. This hierarchy of loves is tested in any number of scenarios. For instance, a couple's adult child may reject their Catholic upbringing and marry outside the Church. Here, loving God above all others may require parents to abstain from participating or acknowledging the marriage, since it is not a marriage in the eyes of God. In another case, a young couple may need to select godparents from among their friends because the couple's siblings are not practicing Catholics. In yet other cases, one spouse may have to challenge the other spouse to spend more time with the family, instead of devoting so much time to a parish ministry. Love has to be ordered and proportionate in a way that respects the hierarchy of loves that Jesus describes.

Question(s) / Prayer

Lord, when we are tempted to place ourselves or others before you, remind us that the first and greatest commandment is to love you with all of our heart, soul, mind, and strength. When we crave human respect or acceptance, help us not to give in to preferring those lesser goods to remaining faithful to you. And grant us the consolation of your Holy Spirit, who is our advocate and guide.

THIRTY-SECOND SUNDAY IN ORDINARY TIME—YEAR B

GOSPEL: MARK 12:38-44

Meditation

The poor widow's meager contribution of two small coins is praised by the Lord. Her remarkable generosity has been lauded by believers through the ages. And yet St. Thomas Aquinas notes that while the poor widow is generous, she is lacking in the virtue of liberality, which is the generous giving of large sums of money. Of course, this is not the poor widow's fault, since only the rich can practice this virtue. But the virtue of liberality reminds us that with material blessings come weighty responsibilities to be generous in a sacrificial way. Those who practice liberality understand that their money is not theirs in the ultimate sense—everything is God's gift. They do not see themselves as "self-made" since they realize that they did not will themselves into existence and thus cannot claim complete autonomy from the Lord and giver of life. The disposition of those who practice liberality is freeing, since it permits them to be lavish in their giving. They find their riches in the practice of virtue.

Question(s) / Prayer

Lord, help us to be generous in all things. And if you have blessed us with material riches, help us to be good stewards of your blessings and to give sacrificially to those who need our help. May our liberality not be simply monetary. May we see the many needs others have of our time and our talent. Grace us with the courage to experience the freedom that comes from giving lavishly.

THIRTY-THIRD SUNDAY IN ORDINARY TIME—YEAR B

GOSPEL: MARK 13:24-32

Meditation

The apocalyptic tone of today's gospel passage is typical of readings used at the end of the liturgical year. With the First Sunday of Advent looming, which is the beginning of the new liturgical year, the Church closes out the current year with readings that express the finality and definitive judgement of the world when Christ returns in glory. This theme has inspired musical compositions like the *Dies Irae* (Day of Wrath) and frescoes such as *The Last Judgement* by Michelangelo, found in the Sistine Chapel in Rome. It seems that in yesteryear, Catholics were much more aware of and sensitive to the end times. A spiritual malaise of a post-modern era is the conviction that there is no sin, no judgement, and no need for repentance. If that is true, then there is no need for Jesus, who came to redeem and save us! In the current paradigm, individuals rely too heavily on the subjectivism of "feeling good" about themselves. Hence, they pay little heed to what God demands of them since God has been supplanted by the ego. This cannot be the attitude of Christ's followers. The *Dies Irae* should not be a time of fright or despair. Instead, believers will rejoice that God's justice reigns. This means that every wrong will be set aright, and that the just will receive their reward while the evil receive their punishment.

Question(s) / Prayer

How aware of and sensitive are we to the Lord's return in glory? Do we take this cataclysmic event seriously? Do we presume our salvation when the business of judgement begins? Have we crafted rationalizations for our compromises with sin? Are we moved to repentance now, while there is still time?

The meditation for the Thirty-Fourth Sunday of Ordinary Time (Solemnity of Christ the King) is found below in the section "Solemnities and Feast Days of the Lord in Ordinary Time."

SUNDAYS IN ORDINARY TIME—YEAR C

SECOND SUNDAY IN ORDINARY TIME—YEAR C

GOSPEL: JOHN 2:1-11

Meditation

The wine steward and the servants take a massive risk in following the Lord's command to fill the wine jars with water. Their faith is rewarded with the Lord's first recorded miracle. Similarly, marriage contains its own risks: the risk that one or both of the spouses will not keep their vows; the risk that the couple may grow apart; and ultimately, the risk that the marriage may not endure. Knowing this, the Lord elevates natural marriage (symbolized by the water) to the dignity of a sacrament (symbolized by the wine). God knows that in order for married persons to remain married in Christ, the couple requires grace to endure, let alone flourish. Of course, grace alone is not a panacea for all troubles that a couple will face, but it is the difference-maker that can keep a marriage together when the storms arrive. Grace is designed to build upon and perfect nature, so it is incumbent on married persons to be intentional and deliberate in their efforts to enrich and cultivate their sacrament. A couple that is not growing in virtue together is a couple that is treading water, increasing the risk of tragedy. The faith of the wine steward and the servants ought to remind all married couples not only to do whatever Jesus tells them, but to take on the risk of letting Christ direct their married love.

Question(s) / Prayer

Father, whenever we are tempted to be self-reliant in order to help our marriage grow, may we be reminded of the faith of the wine steward and the servants, who were so willing to let the Lord lead the effort to bring to fulfillment the good work he had begun in them. May we find ourselves doing whatever your Son instructs us to do, placing our trust in him, and not ourselves. Help us to be intentional and deliberate in cultivating our sacrament, confident that grace can perfect our wounded nature and direct us to lives of holiness.

THIRD SUNDAY IN ORDINARY TIME—YEAR C

GOSPEL: LUKE 1:1-4; 4:14-21

Meditation

After the Exodus, one of the ways that the Jews marked time was the use of the Jubilee system. In its microcosmic form, the Jubilee was celebrated every week with the Sabbath (Saturday). It was not only a day of rest (imitating God's rest from the work of creation narrated in the Book of Genesis); it was also intended for the Jews to gather in prayer to recall God's blessing in delivering them from the bondage of slavery in Egypt during the time of Moses. Every seven years was a Sabbath year (from which we get the idea of a sabbatical)—a year marked with celebrations to commemorate the same realities. Every seven of these Sabbath years (after forty-nine years), the Jews would take off an entire year (year fifty) to remember and celebrate the Great Jubilee. The land was to lie fallow; slaves would be set free; the Jews would return to their ancestral lands associated with their tribal affiliation; and all debts would be cancelled. In today's Gospel, Jesus refers to himself as THE Great Jubilee. He himself is the one who comes to set humanity free from sin and eternal death and restore sight to the spiritually blind. Most importantly, he is the anointed of God (the Christ) upon whom the Holy Spirit rests. Christ is the center and Lord of all history.

Question(s) / Prayer

Father in heaven, grant us the grace to seek the jubilee moments in our marriage: to make time to go on retreat as individuals and as a couple; to cancel all debts of unforgiveness and grudges; and to set one another free from the guilt of unmet expectations or petty bickering. Aid us in our desire to regain spiritual insight, perhaps lost by negligence or indifference. Help us to rediscover the beauty and depth of our Catholic faith and to draw near to you in the Eucharist. May we experience the freedom of these jubilee moments time and again throughout the course of our marriage.

FOURTH SUNDAY IN ORDINARY TIME—YEAR C

GOSPEL: LUKE 4:21-30

Meditation

In the continuation of last Sunday's Gospel, Jesus is expelled from his home synagogue for his provocative words that anger the Jews, who are insulted at the Lord's suggestion that salvation is not only for them, but for the whole world. Jesus cites Gentile biblical heroes in order to reveal to his hearers that God intends their salvation as well. The Jews take umbrage at Jesus' claim and intend to kill him. As only God can, Jesus shows his power and authority over them by eluding their evil designs, since it is only the Lord who determines when he lays down his life. No one takes his life from him unless he gives permission. And although the Lord remains undeterred in his commitment to his mission to save us, we can only conjecture that this rejection at home was a moment of great suffering for him. The rejection was so profound that from this moment on, Jesus would change his base of operations from Nazareth to Capernaum, by the Sea of Galilee. It is at the synagogue in Capernaum that the Lord would teach on the Eucharist in John 6.

Question(s) / Prayer

What are the rejections, big and small, that exist within our marriage: The times when we take each other for granted? A failure to acknowledge even those small kindnesses that make marriage to the other person a true joy? The offhand, insensitive, and careless comment that triggers deep wounds within the other? A larger rejection, such as pressure to deny one another's fertility and succumb to the contraceptive culture around us? In each of these rejections, may we turn to the Lord for compassion and understanding, as he himself faced deep rejection. And may we be quick to apologize for the times when we are the source of rejection within our marriage.

FIFTH SUNDAY IN ORDINARY TIME—YEAR C

GOSPEL: LUKE 5:1-11

Meditation

In the aftermath of the stunning miracle of the miraculous draught of fish, Peter's reaction is telling. Luke writes that "he fell at the knees of Jesus" and asked the Lord to depart from him, for he acknowledged his sin. Peter would only have had this reaction had he known he was in the presence of God. And why? Because Jesus of Nazareth, a carpenter, came crashing into his world and did Peter's job (fishing) better than he could! Luke goes on to indicate that fear and astonishment seized all of those who witnessed what Jesus had done. This was not a lucky coincidence or magic trick. Notice, too, that Peter addresses Jesus as "Master" prior to the miracle. After the miracle, he calls him "Lord." That act of faith denotes that Peter has come to believe that Jesus is Lord and because of that fact, he knows he is unworthy to be in his holy presence. But Jesus will not scold Peter. Instead, he raises him up so that Peter can abandon his trade and follow him. This was the day that changed everything for Peter. By simply giving Jesus a little room in his boat, Jesus transformed his life forever.

Question(s) / Prayer

Are we prepared to allow Jesus on board the boat of our individual lives and of our marriage? Or are we still waiting for that spiritual breakthrough moment in our lives and in our marriage because we hesitate to give him room? And if we give him room, are we prepared for the consequences of what might happen if Jesus comes crashing through into the world that we know and are comfortable operating in? Or do we remain cynical and unmoved—perhaps a bit skeptical about whether grace can transform us? Is there room for Jesus, and if so—how much?

SIXTH SUNDAY IN ORDINARY TIME—YEAR C

GOSPEL: LUKE 6:17, 20-26

Meditation

Luke's presentation of the Beatitudes is markedly shorter than the parallel passage found in Matthew 5, and in Luke the Beatitudes are followed by a series of "woes" or warnings to the self-satisfied and superficial. Jesus is less concerned about one's material wealth and much more concerned about the attitudes and dispositions that riches and "having it all" in this world can foster. These attitudes can engender a sense of self-reliance, presumption, and arrogance. They can also condition someone to place the garnering of human respect above remaining righteous and upright in the sight of God. For some, it is presuming their salvation because they have done well materially in this world or feel comfortable and self-satisfied. For others, it's an outlook on life that deludes them into thinking that, because they have amassed wealth and "life is good," they really don't need God or his life of grace communicated through the sacraments. And for yet others, it is far more important to seem "acceptable" or "pleasing" to men, rather than to live virtuously in the eyes of God. They are hesitant to give credible witness to a life in Christ because it is not the trendy or popular posture among those with whom one wants to curry favor.

Question(s) / Prayer

Do these "woes" apply to us? Do we have the self-awareness to see how self-reliance, presumption, and arrogance are folly? Do we understand that we cannot save ourselves and that God will save or condemn us on his terms and not our own? Would we be prepared now to give an accounting of how we have kept all of his moral commands and not simply the ones that we like, or that are more convenient? Does having deficits in this area concern us enough to move us to repent?

SEVENTH SUNDAY IN ORDINARY TIME—YEAR C

GOSPEL: LUKE 6:27-38

Meditation

Jesus says that "the measure with which you measure will be measured out to you." This warning is paired with prohibitions against condemning others and the exhortation to be forgiving. These are absolutely necessary attitudes and dispositions to have a fruitful and happy marriage. It is very easy for spouses to take each other for granted, which can lead to contempt for one another. How sad it is to hear spouses complain about each other, when so much of the complaining is either hypocritical or about very unimportant matters. It can create a posture of defensiveness, tension, and needless worry that makes one spouse walk on eggshells for fear that the other is so easily offended and bothered by the smallest matter. Spouses begin to grow distant and cold, almost indifferent to each other. By contrast, Jesus' exhortations are intended to create an atmosphere of understanding, gentleness, patience, and mercy. These qualities are lacking in so many marriages and human relationships in general that the litmus test for one's reputation is that one is simply considered "nice." But being nice is not enough, since it is quite possible to be an evil person and yet "nice" to those with whom it may be convenient or expedient to get along (which is quite manipulative). Instead, Jesus calls us to charity: self-sacrificing love forged in the fire of mercy and oriented to a life in him.

Question(s) / Prayer

Lord, help us to remove any bitterness, harshness, impatience, bickering, complaining, and negativity, which can creep into our marriage and cause needless division. Come to our aid in discerning what our real issues are so that we can address them with courage, honesty, and compassion. May we never be found lacking in generosity with one another, especially in a generosity of patience, which paves a path for mildness and joy in living out our vocation.

EIGHTH SUNDAY IN ORDINARY TIME—YEAR C

GOSPEL: LUKE 6:39-45

Meditation

The last phrase in today's Gospel provides an insight into the human condition. Jesus says that "from the fullness of the heart the mouth speaks" (Luke 6:45). This statement is preceded by the well-known analogy of a tree and its corresponding fruit. In other words, good trees produce good fruit and bad trees produce bad fruit. Jesus then continues, "A good person out of the store of goodness in his heart produces good, but an evil person out of a store or evil produces evil..." (Lk 6:45). Here we can observe the need to grow in virtue and to eliminate all vice (sin) from our lives. This is particularly important in a marriage, since one spouse's virtues and vices have a direct impact (for good or ill) on the other (and the children). There is no hiding in marriage. And when vice takes over and hurtful and malicious words spew out of that place of darkness, trouble lurks. Spouses, then, are tasked with helping each other to grow in every virtue and eschew the facile and lazy attitude of "That's just the way I am." No! A lack of progress means regress. There is no middle ground.

Question(s) / Prayer

Father, please help us to recommit ourselves daily to pursuing a life of virtue—to seeking your will and your way in all things. Grant us the grace to put aside ambivalence, laziness, and lukewarmness to welcome the fire of your Spirit into our marriage, to seek the more excellent way of love that your Son provided for us in the Cross. May we never be satisfied with our "progress" since even this is but a participation in your perfection.

NINTH SUNDAY IN ORDINARY TIME—YEAR C
GOSPEL: LUKE 7:1-10

Meditation

The words of the centurion are forever memorialized in the Mass: "Lord, I am not worthy that you should enter under my roof, but only say the word and my soul shall be healed." Not only is the centurion's humble faith remarkable, it is clear from the passage that he was beloved by the Jews for having helped them construct their synagogue in Capernaum. This would have been highly unusual, as the Jews generally had contempt for the Romans and disassociated themselves from their occupiers. Here we see a remarkable relationship, which Jesus will reward with a requested cure. This centurion is lauded by the Lord for having faith greater than any of the Jews he had encountered, which would also have been scandalous. After all, for many of the Jews, the only good Roman was a dead one. In this scene, the "enemy" is the hero.

Question(s) / Prayer

In an age of extreme polarization, are we like Jesus, who sees beyond mere human categories? Are we prepared to be surprised by who our modern-day heroes might be? Or have we written off individuals we know, even if they are making sincere efforts to seek and know the Lord? Are we willing to extend ourselves beyond what is comfortable to bring them to Jesus?

TENTH SUNDAY IN ORDINARY TIME—YEAR C
GOSPEL: LUKE 7:11-17

Meditation

The son of the widow of Naim, along with Jairus's daughter and Lazarus of Bethany are the three persons the Lord revived in the Gospels. Each of these three, however, would die again. This distinguishes resuscitation/revival from resurrection, which is a different dimension of existence wherein the resurrected person no longer dies. This scene foreshadows not only the resurrection but also the scene depicted in Michelangelo's famous *Pieta*, in which our Lady holds the deceased Jesus right after the Crucifixion. In this case, Jesus hands the son of the widow of Naim back to his mother alive. In the case of our Lady, she would receive the Lord's tortured body in death. One can only imagine how the Lord felt at this moment of the handing over of the revived son, when he would not bestow this joy to our Lady until Easter Sunday morning. This ought to widen our understanding of the Lord's humanity—that he had true human feelings. So often, the focus is upon how the beneficiaries of miracles react. Here, we ought to consider how the Lord perceived this foreshadowing of his own death and the bittersweet experience this moment must have brought him.

Question(s) / Prayer

Do we tend to diminish the Lord's humanity, as if he was some superman from antiquity? Do we trust that the Lord knows the human experience intimately, with all of its joys and struggles in all things but sin? Can we entrust our human experience to the Lord, who heals its deficits and makes us whole? Do we go to him in prayer, bringing to him all that burdens us? Or do we tend to think of the Lord as being emotionally aloof, unconcerned with our seemingly "little" lives? Do we realize that he is as close as our breath and that we only need to invoke him to feel his closeness?

ELEVENTH SUNDAY IN ORDINARY TIME—YEAR C

GOSPEL: LUKE 7:36–8:3

Meditation

The interplay between the Lord and the Pharisees should cause couples and individuals to ask if they delude themselves into a false sense of righteousness, assuring themselves that as long as they feel "good" or "positive" as to "where they are in life" they have nothing to worry about in front of God's judgement seat. This type of presumptuous attitude sounds like the Pharisees, who saw no pressing need for ongoing conversion and repentance based on their self-estimation of their standing before God. Couples and individuals should want to assume the posture of the sinful woman, who was forgiven much because she loved the Lord and wanted to conform her life to his. She teaches couples and individuals to pray with desperation before the Lord, and to avoid "praying" with a presumptuous spirit. She emerges as the heroine in the story because she recognized the truth about herself before the Lord and turned to him with confidence in his mercy. This can only happen when the Lord, not one's ego, is at the center of one's life.

Question(s) / Prayer

Lord, teach us the humility of the sinful woman! Help us to avoid all presumption and self-righteousness by helping us to evaluate our lives from your vantage point, not our own. Grant us the insight to see what is uncomfortable but truthful about our marriage and our personal relationship(s) with you. And grant us, Lord, the courage to change what requires conversion in our marriage so that we are truly righteous in your eyes and not merely our own.

TWELFTH SUNDAY IN ORDINARY TIME—YEAR C

GOSPEL: LUKE 9:18-24

Meditation

The question that Jesus puts to his disciples is a question he puts to every believer: "Who do you say that I am?" Lk 9:20). There is an objective answer, known through revelation, that Jesus is Lord—he is the Son of God. But each believer must render a subjective answer to the same question. In other words, who is Jesus in my life? That is more personal and more demanding. It is only when the subjective answer aligns with the objective answer that sanctity begins. It is all too easy to "fit" Jesus into our own world, instead of allowing ourselves to enter into his. In this type of subjectivism, Jesus isn't Lord—the human person is . . . and that is no recipe for salvation. The difference between a saint and a sinner is that a saint knows they are a sinner and they come to the Lord wanting to conform their lives to his in faith. Saints are not born—they are forged out of the cross of discipleship, but that can only begin if the individual human person seeks that alignment between the objective and subjective answers to the very powerful question the Gospel presents today.

Question(s) / Prayer

How do I/we answer the question regarding who Jesus is? Do we attempt to fit Jesus into our worldview, or are we prepared to assimilate ourselves into his? Who is Lord in our lives—Jesus or ourselves? Do we recognize that our egos may be the points of reference in our lives? Do we accept the Lord on his terms or simply on our own—picking and choosing whatever pleases us?

THIRTEENTH SUNDAY IN ORDINARY TIME—YEAR C

GOSPEL: LUKE 9:51-62

Meditation

Today's Gospel contains an assortment of three vignettes that appear to be separate scenes in the Lord's life, each containing its own message. In the first instance, the Lord rebukes James and John for their vengeful request to smite unbelieving Samaritans (blood enemies of the Jews). Jesus' response reminds us that faith cannot be forced or coerced. It must be the response of a free individual who desires friendship with the Lord. In the second and third instances, the Lord reminds us that he takes second place to no one and that his followers must be prepared to accept the hardships that will come with authentic discipleship. Those hardships may include a lack of security, creature comforts, and the esteem of men. And the priority that Jesus insists upon having in the lives of his followers must even supersede their allegiance to their family. It is a radical call to follow the Lord, but it must be accepted in freedom, faith, and love (not in the blind obedience that fundamentalists and radicals often insist upon). The Lord knows that loving him will make big demands of his followers, but he promises much more than any human person can—eternal glory and salvation.

Question(s) / Prayer

Lord, grant us the grace to choose you freely in faith. May we always trust your desire to shape and form us in your own image and likeness, loyal to the will of the Father. May we embrace the hardships that discipleship will require of us, always rejoicing that those who remain faithful have their names written in heaven. And may we never presume our salvation either—always returning to you in humble prayer, knowing that we are in constant need of discernment and your guidance.

FOURTEENTH SUNDAY IN ORDINARY TIME—YEAR C

GOSPEL: LUKE 10:1-12, 17-20

Meditation

Jesus gives a somewhat surprising exhortation to his disciples as to how to conduct themselves when they meet opposition in spreading the Gospel. He instructs them to employ a dramatic gesture—shaking the dust off of *their* feet in testimony against their opponents. This brings into focus some important considerations regarding the life of a follower of the Lord: First, we ought to expect opposition to spreading the Gospel. The question is not if, but when. Second, we must accept that there are limits to what we can do propose the Gospel. Very often, we can become very frustrated in wanting another person's conversion more than they want it for themselves. And we start to believe that their conversion is mostly contingent on our efforts. In reality, it is the Lord who moves hearts by grace. Our task is to sow the seed, cultivate growth, and remove obstacles that we are able to clear out. But how hearts are converted is always mysterious and graced, often beyond mere human comprehension. Third, we are not tasked with watering down or adjusting the message of the Gospel to placate our hearers. Capitulations and compromises of the truth are never rooted in true charity, for the Lord did not come to be changed by the world, but to change it and redeem it back to the Father.

Question(s) / Prayer

Are we engaged in our baptismal call to be prophetic in the world? Are we accepting the challenge to reach out to those whom we can influence? Do we recognize the limits of what we can do, knowing that all is graced participation in the Lord's work? Do we act as if everything depends on us and that God only makes up for what we lack? Do we use our limits as an excuse for avoiding the demands of our prophetic office?

FIFTEENTH SUNDAY IN ORDINARY TIME—YEAR C

GOSPEL: LUKE 10:25-37

Meditation

In the words of the ancient Christian writer Origen, the Parable of the Good Samaritan is an allegory for salvation history: The man who falls into the hands of robbers is symbolic of Adam. The descent from Jerusalem to Jericho is symbolic of going from heaven down to earth (an allegory for Adam's life on earth as a gift from God). The robbers are the Devil and his minions. The wounds are the effects of Original Sin. The priest and the Levite who pass by represent the Law and the Prophets, who are unable to heal the man. The Good Samaritan is Christ, who puts the man on his beast (the Cross) after dressing his wounds with oil and wine (Baptism and the Eucharist) and carries him to the inn (the Church) manned by the innkeeper (St. Peter). The payment of two coins is symbolic of Christ's humanity and divinity paid for our redemption, and his promise of return is symbolic of the Last Judgement. To add to the splendor of this allegory, St. Luke immortalizes the Samaritan as the hero, which would have been objectionable to a Jewish audience, who regarded Samaritans as their blood enemies. For a Jew, the only good Samaritan was a dead one. Moreover, the parable is not merely an exhortation to love one's neighbor, but it directly answers the question put to Jesus: "Who is my neighbor?" (Lk 10:29) And the answer is: everybody.

Question(s) / Prayer

Lord, help us to help those who are the most difficult to love, knowing that you also died for them as well. May we give without counting the cost and even pray for our enemies. Help us to strive for Christian perfection by internalizing your command to love those who do not love us, even if that means simply willing their good in a dispassionate manner.

SIXTEENTH SUNDAY IN ORDINARY TIME—YEAR C

GOSPEL: LUKE 10:38-42

Meditation

Martha and Mary are often considered as emblems of the active life and contemplative life, respectively. While the Church esteems the latter over the former, the contemplative life seems difficult to grasp for laypersons in the world. After all, very few have luxury of living a contemplative life when the demands of work, family, and school pull in the opposite direction. Perhaps the invitation for laypersons is to become active-contemplatives. In other words, a follower of Jesus in the world must engage the world and excel therein, all the way maintaining a contemplative spirit rooted in prayer. Rather than chose between the contemplative life and the active life, the Gospel invites ordinary people to live both walks of life in tandem, so that the active life can be animated by and receive its cues from the contemplative spirit that every follower should create by resolving that when their godly needs are met, they can work to serve those in most need.

Question(s) / Prayer

What can we do to strive to live active-contemplative lives? Are we too easily given to the heresy of activism, whereby a person's worth is determined by their productivity or capacity to work? Do we cultivate a contemplative spirit as we go about our activity, or do we tend to keep the two areas of our lives separate?

SEVENTEENTH SUNDAY IN ORDINARY TIME—YEAR C

GOSPEL: LUKE 11:1-13

Meditation

Today's gospel passage teaches us not only to ask for divine favors, but *what* favors to ask for and *how* to ask for them. For instance, the Lord's Prayer is composed of seven petitions. Each of the petitions indicates what we should ask for—those things that really matter to God. So often, we find ourselves asking for things or favors that are not essential to our salvation or perhaps miss the mark as to God's priorities for us. Hence, the Our Father teaches us to ask that God's name be made holy in us; that his Kingdom and will be done his way; for our spiritual food; for forgiveness of our sins; and for preservation from temptation and sin. It is helpful to consider what we ask for and whether or not these requests align with what God has on his priority list for us, as indicated by the Lord's Prayer. Moreover, the Gospel passage teaches us *how* to ask for divine favors—the proper dispositions we ought to have in our requests. The remainder of the passage teaches us to ask with perseverance, with trust in the answer God wants to give, and with sincerity in our requests. If we ask as a child asks their father for a favor and not as a consumer who turns to God as a service provider, we begin to learn to receive all that he gives us as gift.

Question(s) / Prayer

Do we ask the Lord for the most important things to him, as opposed to our own priorities? Are our requests made with our salvation in mind, or are our requests myopic and too worldly? Do we ask with sincerity and confidence as a child asks their father? Are we prepared to accept the Lord's answer to our prayers even if that answer is "no" or "not yet," fully trusting that even a negative answer is always a positive gift from him?

EIGHTEENTH SUNDAY IN ORDINARY TIME—YEAR C

GOSPEL: LUKE 12:13-21

Meditation

Jesus' words challenge the pervading materialism that permeates the mindsets and worldviews of a not insignificant number of people today. This is not merely the problem of the rich. Even the poor can be consumed with money and acquiring material possessions. But this materialism is not merely defined by greed or a preoccupation with possessing material goods. It goes deeper. Another dimension of materialism is the implicit belief that as long as human persons have their basic material human needs met (food, water, clothing, shelter, security), they are living a good life. But this impoverished perspective ignores the spiritual dimension of man, which is the part of him which is most like God. Materialistic persons are in constant pursuit of fulfillment, which they believe "things" or "experiences" can provide. And the pursuit never ends because only God can truly fill that void present in every human person wounded by Original Sin. Here, Jesus challenges us to become rich in those things that matter to God and to avoid becoming defined by our "net worth" or material success. It's as unpopular a message today as it was in the time of the Lord. Followers of the Lord may grasp this simple truth cognitively, but the will is so often weakened by the lure of materialism.

Question(s) / Prayer

How do we define "living a good life"? Is our attitude or mind-set secular or Christian? Are we too given to the material, so that we ignore or downplay the importance of the spiritual? Do our riches tempt us the very self-satisfaction that the Gospel warns against? How invested are we in the things that matter to God? Are we prepared to re-orient ourselves to him?

NINETEENTH SUNDAY IN ORDINARY TIME—YEAR C

GOSPEL: LUKE 12:32-48

Meditation

In a very stern parable, the Lord warns against the sin of presumption, a serious spiritual malaise that plagues many believers and would-be believers. Presumption takes many forms: For some, it is the assumption that one will always "have more time" for conversion and interior growth. For others, it is the erroneous self-estimation that as long as "I don't kill anybody" I have no need for conversion or change. And for others, it is the vapid claim that when we die, we all go "to some better place." This is fodder for the feeble-minded and weak of resolve. But there is more. Jesus also specifies the types of responsibilities individuals bear for having been given greater gifts. In sum, those who are blessed with more are expected to do more and are held to a higher standard. This is precisely why Jesus then says that from those to whom much is given, much more is expected. When one lives a comfortable life, it is very easy to be lulled into self-satisfaction and *acedia* (spiritual boredom). The parable moves us to have a sense of urgency and a spirit of spiritual vigilance so as to be found well prepared to meet the master.

Question(s) / Prayer

What are our spiritual blind spots of presumption? Are we prepared to make an honest assessment according to the standards by which we think Jesus will judge us by? Or are our standards self-styled? Do we maintain a spirit of vigilance to guard our lives of faith and keep the flame of love for the Lord alive?

TWENTIETH SUNDAY IN ORDINARY TIME—YEAR C

GOSPEL: JOHN 12:49-53

Meditation

With its uncomfortable message, today's Gospel paints an often-painful reality for sincere followers of the Lord. It's important to understand that the Lord does not actively will division among family and friends. However, he both predicted it and allows it to happen. Jesus has always known that following him in fidelity will cause division when not all of one's family or circle of friends are faithful as well. There can be spoken and unspoken tensions, avoidance of others, and outright confrontations and disputes. Whenever a disciple experiences this heartache, today's Gospel should be of tremendous consolation. Even our Lord himself was not exempt from this rejection.

On a more positive note, how beautifully refreshing it is to experience families and friends who are first and foremost friends of the Lord. There is an intimacy and closeness among such persons because they are living in the freedom and glory of the children of God. That is not to say that their lives are devoid of the Cross. But each cross in their lives is understood within the context of the Lord's life in which they participate.

Question(s) / Prayer

Lord, help us to remain strong in your love—especially when that puts us at odds with family members and friends who do not know or truly love you, even if they style themselves faithful disciples. Help us to understand that we are participating in one of the heavier crosses that you yourself endured. We know that you wish us to be unified, but only unified in you. Help us to eschew illusory "unity" under a false "peace" that lacks integrity, all the while maintaining a spirit of charity for those who are far from you. May we never be a hindrance or obstacle to their discipleship.

TWENTY-FIRST SUNDAY IN ORDINARY TIME—YEAR C

GOSPEL: LUKE 13:22-30

Meditation

If one is paying close attention to today's Gospel, there is something quite sobering about it: Jesus distinguishes between those who know about him and those who personally know him through a life of faith, obedience to his moral law, and good works. The persons whom Jesus rejects as being unknown to him do maintain an affiliation with him, however loosely. In modern terms, these might be persons who sent their children to Catholic school, attended Mass from time to time but always on Christmas and Easter, prayed occasionally, were generous to the poor when it was convenient, and always thought of themselves as at least culturally Catholic. The gospel passage suggests that this is not nearly enough. Jesus doesn't want followers with a nominal or loose affiliation with him (or the institutions of the Church). No, the Lord desires true and committed disciples whose lives are completely oriented towards him, especially in those areas that are most challenging. Those who believe that it is sufficient to be Catholic in name only but live lives that are not completely with Jesus ought never to presume their salvation. Following the Lord is not for the faint of heart. It requires an abiding and genuine commitment rooted in love, not mere "good enough" sufficiency, which ends up being quite insufficient.

Question(s) / Prayer

Lord, help us to know learn and know our Catholic faith so that we can have true insight into what you expect of those whom you will save. May we never presume our salvation, based on an uncommitted affiliation that was never rooted in love of you, but was motivated by a checklist that we deemed would be sufficient signs of "discipleship." Grant us the grace not only to know about you but to know you yourself through our personal experience of your love poured into our souls through the sacraments.

TWENTY-SECOND SUNDAY IN ORDINARY TIME—YEAR C

GOSPEL: LUKE 14:1,7-14

Meditation

As in many cultures, meals in Jewish culture were much more than opportunities to eat. Meals meant community-building, family bonding, and the preservation of cultural norms and practices. Jesus often used meals as settings to teach, as is the case in today's gospel passage. In the first instance, he extols the high premium God places on humility and the importance of never assuming one's status—especially in the eyes of the Father. What an important lesson to heed in an age of presumption, narcissism, and self-promotion—hyper-accelerated by social media trending and attention-seeking.

In the second instance, the Lord impresses upon his hosts the need to never neglect the poor and marginalized of the community. Helping those who cannot repay you in this life helps build a very important credit line for eternal life, as Jesus will expound upon in Matthew 25. "Whatever you did for one of these least brothers of mine, you did for me" (Mt 25:40). It is quite easy to become preoccupied with one's orbit to the neglect of so many persons who have real needs. And yet Christian charity has always been exercised with a preferential option for the poor. It is refreshingly impressive to see couples and families commit time and resources to assist the indigent. It shows a real dedication to those so beloved to the Lord! Fewer things move one outside of one's own "world" and help cultivate a culture of genuine compassion and mercy.

Question(s) / Prayer

Father, may we never presume our status before you, save that we are your beloved children. Help us to recall that this status alone is not enough to secure our salvation. Rather, help us to dedicate or rededicate ourselves to the care of the poor, however we are able to assist. May we avoid the temptation to assign this responsibility to others. May we take care of those whom we can reach and encourage others to do the same, all in your name.

TWENTY-THIRD SUNDAY IN ORDINARY TIME—YEAR C

GOSPEL: LUKE 14:25-33

Meditation

Jesus praises the virtue of prudence, the cardinal virtue regarded as the charioteer of all the virtues. It's the virtue that helps us to discern clearly the right thing to do at the right time and for the right reason. It's also the virtue that helps us to practice all of the other virtues well and in an ordered manner. Hence, it is not enough to be loving or courageous or just—one must practice these virtues in accord with the moral law of God and in a way most pleasing to him. In popular culture, prudence is praised when it involves financial matters. Unfortunately, prudence is derided when it comes to sexual morality. But in the Christian life, prudence is always praised. It helps to regulate our zeal for righteousness and to navigate through the often-complicated web of modern living and attitudes that make advancing the Gospel quite difficult at times. Notice that the examples Jesus uses to demonstrate the importance of prudence range from family affairs to business projects to military strategy to personal finances. This wide range of examples shows that all of human affairs must be directed to the Lord. There is nothing outside of his purview or governance. Compartmentalizing dimensions of one's life and segregating them from God is a fool's errand and immensely imprudent. He desires to be all in all, if only we allow him.

Question(s) / Prayer

In what segments of our lives do we tend to keep Jesus at bay? Is he our welcomed guest in all dimensions of our lives? Do we keep him out of the picture when it comes to sexual ethics or how we use money or any other dimension of life that we are unwilling to relinquish to him? Do we imprudently think that we can place anything or anyone above the Lord and be his genuine disciple?

TWENTY-FOURTH SUNDAY IN ORDINARY TIME—YEAR C

GOSPEL: LUKE 15:1-32

Meditation

Both images found in today's Gospel (the lost sheep and the lost coin) depict the premium God places on repentance. Repentance implies a change of mind and a reorientation of perspective. But this change of mind or perspective is not self-generated. Notice in the parable that it requires the intervention of the shepherd or the woman sweeping the house. In other words, repentance is rooted in grace, which is omnipresent to anyone who desires it. Herein lies the challenge: Neither the lost sheep nor the lost coin knew it was lost. Both needed to be discovered or found in order to be saved. This is an often overlooked dimension of Christian discipleship—it is more about being found by God than about our seeking him. God is always seeking us, but we can often resist him and hide behind all kinds of relationships, things, ambitions, and sins. Authentic discipleship requires a desire (itself already a grace) to be found. And how is one found? By an honest admission of the need to reform, to repent, to confess sin, and to be absolved. It all starts with a thorough and sincere examination of conscience taken from God's perspective and not merely our own. After all, sin can only be truly understood through his eyes. And when we are found, there is great rejoicing in heaven.

Question(s) / Prayer

What keeps us from being found? Do we see ourselves as a lost sheep or lost coin in need of being discovered? Do we see our need for ongoing conversion and the confession of our sins? Are we too proud to need the shepherd or the woman with broom in hand to find our way back to where we belong? Do we encourage one another on our personal paths to conversion?

TWENTY-FIFTH SUNDAY IN ORDINARY TIME—YEAR C

GOSPEL: LUKE 16:1-13

Meditation

There's a remarkable twist in today's Gospel: the rich man *commended* the dishonest steward for acting prudently, even if that meant that the steward traded on the rich man's credit to create a soft landing for himself after he was fired. It's important to note that Jesus isn't praising the dishonest steward's dishonesty per se. However, he uses this parable to urge his followers to be as cunning about the project of salvation as the worldly are in pursuing their inferior life goals. For all of his crookedness, the steward exhibited three virtues worth highlighting. First, the dishonest steward had good *self-awareness*. Citing his limitations (lack of physical strength, too much pride to beg), he set out to set himself up for the future. Second, the dishonest steward *anticipated* his potential dire straits by making arrangements with his master's creditors. This type of anticipation is needed in the world of discipleship to avoid falling into sin, to "get ahead" of children who are trending away from the Faith, and to answer questions whenever there are challenges made to the Church's authority or in the face of scandals, just to name a couple of examples. The dishonest steward did not simply react in a passive manner. Instead, he got in front of this situation to ensure a better outcome. Third, the dishonest steward acted with a sense of *urgency* (the Gospel uses the word "quickly") to remediate his anticipated problems. Rather than allow circumstances to dictate his future, he moved with alacrity.

Question(s) / Prayer

How do we employ our cleverness in the interest of the Gospel and promoting the cause of Christ? Is the Gospel the kind of "good news" in our lives that we are rarely found promoting, almost embarrassed to be known as being devout or religious? Are we more enthusiastic about our sports teams and our hobbies than we are about things that pertain directly to the Church? Do we have the self-awareness, anticipation, and urgency that make the dishonest steward worthy of the Lord's praise?

TWENTY-SIXTH SUNDAY IN ORDINARY TIME—YEAR C

GOSPEL: LUKE 16:19-31

Meditation

Today's Gospel contains a subtle but important detail that is often overlooked: While the rich man in the parable remains nameless, readers learn the name of Lazarus, the beggar. This was a technique used by ancient writers to communicate the idea that the nameless person was a caricature of the human condition and/or to highlight the identity of the true hero (in this case, Lazarus). Notice, too, that Jesus makes the beggar the hero, which would have been the opposite expectation of his hearers. After all, the wealthy were often the envy of the poor, since they appeared to "have it all." But Jesus contradicts this human stereotype, revealing what matters most to God. It is also important to note that the rich man's sin was not being rich. Rather, his sin was the neglect of the poor man right under his nose. Jesus held no animosity toward the rich. In fact, some of his closest friends (Martha, Mary, and Lazarus of Bethany—not the same as the Lazarus in today's parable) were quite wealthy. Rather, Jesus criticizes the rich who do not see their material blessings as placing upon them a particular responsibility to the poor. This is also known as *noblesse oblige*—the obligation of the nobility towards the indigent and less privileged. The materially rich run the risk of thinking that they are self-made. The reality is that any blessing we have is a participation in God's goodness. We are but stewards of what he gives.

But there is another poverty that requires our attention: spiritual poverty, which can cut across all socio-economic strata. If we reduce "wealth" to material goods, we neglect the supreme importance of spiritual wealth, which can be the possession of any person. Disciples of the Lord are called to be mindful of both the spiritual and corporal works of mercy, which build up those riches in every person.

Question(s) / Prayer

How attentive are we to the needs of the materially poor and of the spiritually poor? Do we recognize any spiritual poverty in our lives, or do we content ourselves with being materially blessed as sufficient? Are there persons "right under our nose" whom we neglect materially or spiritually? How can the corporal and spiritual works of mercy help guide the way in which we address them?

TWENTY-SEVENTH SUNDAY IN ORDINARY TIME—YEAR C

GOSPEL: LUKE 17:5-10

Meditation

The practice of discipleship requires the virtue of humility. After all, a disciple (*discipulus*, in Latin) means "student," which assumes being under the tutelage of a teacher or master. Today's Gospel paints the picture of the type of disposition the Lord expects of his students—to think of themselves as nothing special, especially when they have only done what was required. This is the Christian antidote to the self-congratulatory, narcissistic ethos of the day, which can't help but tell everyone how awesome they are. It's the ethos that excuses self-indulgence because "I deserve it." Instead, students of the Lord attempt to imitate his self-abnegation, the deference of his praise to the Father, and his complete rejection of entitlement or privilege. In order to be "somebody" in Jesus' world, one ought to strive to be "nobody." Saints like John the Baptist always recognized that the while the Lord must increase, they must decrease. And this is the necessary spirit of humility needed to thrive in marriage. The unnoticed kindnesses, the diaper changes at 3:00 a.m. that no one claps for, little efforts to make the lives of others at home just a bit easier, and the gentle and encouraging word of appreciation are the ingredients that please the Lord and help marriages and families thrive.

Question(s) / Prayer

Lord, help us to desire to be your simple and humble servants. When the world tells us to celebrate ourselves, help us to celebrate you. When the world insists that we broadcast all over social media how "wonderful" our lives are, inspire us to seek out those who are struggling without fanfare. When the world tells us we ought to be offended whenever we are not recognized, help us to unite ourselves with you—who never sought his own fame, but the glory of the Father.

TWENTY-EIGHTH SUNDAY IN ORDINARY TIME—YEAR C

GOSPEL: LUKE 17:11-19

Meditation

Even non-religiously-inclined persons can perceive the ingratitude of the nine lepers who failed to thank the Lord for their healing. It's as if this incident was to be predictive of the long history of ingratitude that human persons would show God. For instance, how many Catholics fail to give thanks (interestingly, *eucharistein* is Greek for "thanksgiving") on Sundays by attending Mass, having forgotten the Lord's blessings? Some even go so far as to say, "I don't need to go to Mass to give thanks," even if this obstinacy contradicts divine precept (Catholics observe the Third Commandment by attending Mass). Spiritual forgetfulness is a serious spiritual malaise. It fails to recognize that all blessings flow from the Lord. It can grow into a presumptuous and entitled spirit that incentivizes the human person to live as if God does not exist. It fosters a spirit of ingratitude and pride that fails to acknowledge how utterly dependent each human person is on God for their very existence. It shows a lack of graciousness that even human courtesy and custom require us to practice in everyday living. Saying "thank you" costs us nothing, and yet how few people are willing to say these simple words to one another and to the Lord. When the human person is not oriented to the Lord, the forgetfulness of ingratitude is one of the first signs of egocentrism.

Question(s) / Prayer

Are we all too quick to forget the Lord? Do we repay his blessings by attending Mass, where we can receive him—the blessing of all blessings? When we forget to attend Mass, do we confess our sins before returning to Communion? Or do we forget the gravity of missing Sunday Mass since we have become our own measure and standard of morality? Do we answer to a moral authority higher than ourselves? Or have we forgotten our place?

TWENTY-NINTH SUNDAY IN ORDINARY TIME—YEAR C

GOSPEL: LUKE 18:1-8

Meditation

In today's Gospel, Jesus praises the tenacity and perseverance of the widow and the imperfectly motivated prudence of the dishonest judge. But he issues a dire warning phrased as a question, as a way of impressing upon believers the need for perseverance in prayer. He asks, "When the Son of Man comes, will he find faith on earth?" (Lk 18:8). The question, when considered carefully, is jarring. First, Jesus assures us that he will return to judge the living and the dead. Many people live today as if God does not exist and there is no sin and no judgement. The Lord's words warn us otherwise. Second, Jesus is concerned that very few will persevere in faith and prayer. This reality plagues the Church in the modern era. Observe the free-fall decline of our once glorious Western civilization, imbued by Christian faith. Waning church attendance, the tsunami of secularization, the abandonment of Christian moral principles, and the glorification of materialism should cause one to wonder how many will be saved. And more personally, will we be among them? Presumption of one's salvation is a very serious spiritual disease. The Lord's warning, phrased as a question, suggests how rampant it would be in successive generations of human history.

Question(s) / Prayer

Lord, grant us the tenacity and perseverance of the widow in the parable. Purify our imperfectly motivated prudence to anticipate our particular judgement at our death and the final judgement at the end of time. Help to convert our fear into love, so that we may face these most important moments of our existence with trust in your mercy and reverence for your justice.

THIRTIETH SUNDAY IN ORDINARY TIME—YEAR C

GOSPEL: LUKE 18:9-14

Meditation

Jesus' hearers would have been shocked at the portrayal of the Pharisee and the tax collector depicted in today's gospel passage. Jesus portrays the Pharisees, considered by most Jews to be spiritually elite and on the fast track of ritual purity and righteousness, as presumptuous, arrogant, and brimming with self-righteous pride. Meanwhile, the tax collector is presented as humble, contrite, sincere, and—most importantly—justified before God. This portrayal would have been the exact opposite from the expectations of Jesus' hearers. The parable invites us to consider obvious lessons such as the value of imitating the virtues of the converted tax collector. But it may also teach us more subtle lessons: First, one ought never judge another person's standing before God. Second, conversion is possible for even the most hardened of sinners. Grace is never to be underestimated. Third, it is important to distinguish between external piety and internal conversion and sanctity. It's important never to assume that the externally pious are truly holy. We are often unaware of the burdens under which persons labor and the particular crosses they bear, which remain hidden to us. More than an exhortation not to judge a book by its cover, the parable moves us to attempt to see others as God sees them.

Question(s) / Prayer

Lord, help us to pray like the tax collector. Help us to recognize our sinfulness, our need for mercy, and our lowliness before your majesty. Lift us up in confidence that your mercy heals and restores. Grant us the wisdom to recognize that admitting our sinfulness is not a sign of weakness, but of strength—the strength that comes from your healing grace and mercy.

THIRTY-FIRST SUNDAY IN ORDINARY TIME—YEAR C

GOSPEL: LUKE 19:1-10

Meditation

Traditionally, Zacchaeus has been portrayed as a sinner (since he is a tax collector) in need of conversion. However, the English translation of his dialogue with the Lord is not quite accurate. In reality, Zacchaeus does not say that he SHALL give half of his earnings to the poor or repay those whom he has extorted four times over. In the original Greek, Zacchaeus *already gives and repays* (present indicative tense) now! And yet this present indicative tense suggests future acts of repayment and generosity. In encountering Jesus, Zacchaeus is given the grace of self-awareness, and he seizes the moment. He knows that he must do more! He realizes that salvation incarnate is before him in the person of Jesus. Jesus knows the depths of Zacchaeus's conversion and the joy with which Zacchaeus welcomes him. In light of Zacchaeus' response to the grace of self-awareness, the Lord insists on staying with Zacchaeus in his house—to enter into communion with him.

Question(s) / Prayer

Lord, help us to seize the moment! May we look for you and welcome you wholeheartedly into the "homes" where you have yet to visit in our souls. Might we have the self-awareness of Zacchaeus—that each of us needs conversion and repentance in order to welcome you into the abode of our lives. Help us to remember that this movement begins with your grace—that we cannot simply "move ourselves" to this place but that we are completely dependent on you!

THIRTY-SECOND SUNDAY IN ORDINARY TIME—YEAR C

GOSPEL: LUKE 20:27-38

Meditation

Jesus points to the surpassing excellence of celibacy for the sake of the Kingdom as an objectively superior state of life, above marriage. Celibates live in their bodies now as the gospel passage relates we will all live in heaven (hopefully), where there is neither giving nor taking in marriage. Hence, celibates are a constant witness to married persons of life in the world to come. They have foregone their natural right to marriage in this life as a sign and witness of life in heaven. This is a difficult state of life for many to understand, since most of Western civilization places a premium on coupling. It takes solid Catholic couples and families to understand the meaning and value of celibacy as a charism in the Church. And just as married couples witness to celibates by persevering in their vows, so do celibates witness to married couples by persevering in theirs. When married persons and celibates live their states of life well, the Church flourishes and comes alive.

Question(s) / Prayer

Do we understand the gift of celibacy in the Church? Do we esteem it above marriage itself? Do we encourage our children to pursue this objectively superior state of life with freedom of discernment? Do we speak well of celibates at our family dinner table so that they are honored and respected for the witness they provide for the Church?

THIRTY-THIRD SUNDAY IN ORDINARY TIME—YEAR C

GOSPEL: LUKE 21:5-19

Meditation

Christ's words in today's Gospel offer a stern warning to believers: Persecution and perseverance will be the hallmarks of those who are saved. Believers ought to anticipate persecution for staying faithful to the Lord. Notice that the persecutions may come from civil and religious leaders, fellow believers, parents, relatives, and friends. In other words, believers should anticipate any and all possibilities, including outright hatred and death. These situations will lead to believers giving testimony for their faith. And yet, how many believers will buckle under the pressure? Fidelity is not for the weak or faint of heart. In the current ethical paradigm, many believers crumble under the pressure to accept all kinds of immoralities within families (e.g., illicit unions of varying kinds), hostility to the Faith, and the accusation of being "too Catholic," and other persecutions that are not even tantamount to experiencing hatred and/or death. Prayer, fasting, and almsgiving are invaluable aids to steeling followers of Christ against the persecutions that come their way, however subtle they may be. Jesus does not instruct his followers to compromise to "keep the peace" either. Instead, he assures us that his words will become our own in defending God's law of love.

Question(s) / Prayer

Lord, whenever we fall into a "soft" discipleship that places no real demands on us, help us to examine whether or not our lack of witness gives others the impression that we have been co-opted into the mindset of our would-be persecutors. And help us, we pray, not to have a martyr complex either—assuming that every contradiction is a persecution. And most importantly, grant us the grace to live in a way that is authentic. Banish from us any temptation to hypocrisy, and heal those divisions that hardness of heart has created.

The meditation for the Thirty-Fourth Sunday of Ordinary Time (Solemnity of Christ the King) is found in the next section, "Solemnities and Feast Days of the Lord in Ordinary Time."

SOLEMNITIES AND FEAST DAYS OF THE LORD IN ORDINARY TIME

FEAST OF THE PRESENTATION OF THE LORD—FEBRUARY 2

GOSPEL: LUKE 2:22-40

Meditation

Forty days after the Nativity, St. Joseph and our Lady take the baby Jesus to the Temple to present him to God, as prescribed by Jewish law. They encounter two elderly persons, Simeon and Anna, both of whom have waited for the day when they could meet the Messiah. Simeon in particular had been told by the Holy Spirit that he "should not see death before he had seen the Messiah of the Lord" (Lk 2:26). Anna, for her part, was an octogenarian. Both saints demonstrate a virtue in short supply in the modern age: patience. In a world of the "instant" it is easy to lose sight of the fact that the cultivation and maturation of a marital relationship take time and perseverance. It requires the forbearance necessary to overcome spousal differences, limitations, and difficulties. It also requires a humble admission that it is not a spouse's responsibility per se to convert the other, especially when that conversion has little to do with the other's sanctity but is a mask for "converting" the other to suit *their* needs and desires—to form them into the spouse they think the other should be. That is not to say that spouses should not pray for each other's conversion, but that prayer should be born out of a genuine desire to help the other person get to heaven. All of this requires patience and perseverance, all the while praying for one's own personal conversion as well.

Question(s) / Prayer

Lord, help us to cultivate deep and abiding patience with ourselves and one another. May we ease the path of patience with quick apologies and genuine forgiveness, so that we can make the journey to the Father's house together and not apart. May we guard against growing apart in the spiritual life, all the while respecting our differences, preferences, and limitations. May we wait on each other, knowing that each person makes progress in the interior life as they are able. Without nagging or pleading, may we learn the "long game" of gentle encouragement, which engenders spiritual freedom and peace.

SOLEMNITY OF THE MOST HOLY TRINITY—FIRST SUNDAY AFTER PENTECOST

GOSPEL: JOHN 3:16-18 (YEAR A) / MATTHEW 28:16-20 (YEAR B) / JOHN 16:12-15 (YEAR C)

Meditation

The Most Holy Trinity is the primordial communion of persons. It provides the pattern and goal for every marriage. Just as the persons of the Trinity love each other without counting the cost and with freedom and intentionality, married persons are called to love one another (and their family) by pouring themselves out for the other. Within the Trinity there is neither selfishness, nor pride, nor harshness. Instead, Trinitarian love is defined by self-sacrifice, mildness, and self-gift. Catholics are constantly reminded of this most fundamental mystery of the Faith—that God is three Persons and the ultimate union of love, especially as we tend to begin all prayers with the sign of the Cross. The Blessed Virgin Mary enjoys a particularly unique relationship to the Trinity: Daughter of the Father, Mother of the Son, Spouse of the Holy Spirit. She is the first and best teacher of what living a life within the bosom of the Trinity ought to look like. Her complete self-gift to allow the Trinity to use her for divine purposes should inspire us to do the same.

Question(s) / Prayer

Do we approach our married lives with a Trinitarian disposition of love? Does the community we share with one another reflect the love of the Trinity? Do we anticipate each other in showing love, or do we prefer to do the least we need to do in order to keep the other minimally happy? By analogy, does our openness to welcoming more children into our family reflect the complete openness of love found within the Trinity? What are the blocks that we place in the way of Trinitarian love in our marriage and family: selfishness, pride, ambivalence, harshness, anger? May our Lady help us to put aside these fallen tendencies, so that we better imitate her virtues and live in the freedom and glory of the children of God.

OR—

Meditation

The Most Holy Trinity is the fundamental mystery of Christian faith. The Trinity is the primordial community of persons. If we are made in the image and likeness of God, then we, too, are called to live in community. Marriage and family life are meant to be reflective of the inner life of the Trinity: individual Persons loving one another and sacrificing for one another without counting the cost. Our call to reflect the dynamics of the Trinity in our lives is the great antidote to the isolation and loneliness that so many feel today. Sadly, even within marriages and families, individuals can silo into their own worlds, often galvanized by the artificiality of social media and the curated "reality" of the smartphone. Couples and families must fight against the tendency towards a lack of cohesion and connection within the marriage and family, often unaware of the derelict effects of the handy devices that become a "necessary" appendage for survival but divide us from the persons who should be closest to us.

Question(s) / Prayer

When was the last time that we took a careful look at our use of technology and its effects on our growth in holiness as a couple and/or family? Do we take seriously the need for genuine human connection or are we satisfied to be alone together? Do we create the space needed to allow the loving world of the Trinity to permeate our world?

SOLEMNITY OF THE MOST HOLY BODY AND BLOOD OF CHRIST (CORPUS CHRISTI)— SUNDAY AFTER THE MOST HOLY TRINITY

GOSPEL: JOHN 6:51-58 (YEAR A) / MARK 14:12-16, 22-26 (YEAR B) / LUKE 9:11B-17 (YEAR C)

Meditation

While it has fallen out of style, many of the traditional dogmatic tractates emphasize the nuptial meaning of the Eucharist. For instance, the person of Jesus is the marriage between divinity and humanity, for he is true God and true man. The Song of Songs in the Old Testament is lyric, erotic poetry about a lover chasing his beloved until she is possessed, symbolic of how God pursues us until we are his. Notably, the meter and verse cadence of the Song of Songs is the pattern for the meter and verse cadence of the Traditional Latin Mass. In many of the churches around the city of Rome, altars are adorned with wedding canopies above them, known as *baldacchinos*. The altar, then, is the wedding bed for the great wedding feast of the Lamb, portrayed in the Book of Revelation. These are but a few examples of the nuptial meaning of the Eucharist, and for most Catholics, they are hidden in plain sight. This should remind us that the Lord is deeply interested in marriage and family, as the primary vehicle through which the Faith is passed down through the generations. When these suffer breakdowns, so does the transmission of the Faith, as we observe in our contemporary culture so replete with divorce and familial dysfunctionality. If the Eucharist, with its nuptial meaning, is the source and summit of the entire Christian life, this principle certainly applies to marriage itself.

Question(s) / Prayer

Lord, grant us the grace to imitate you in your Eucharistic presence: gentle, broken, and spent for others, generous, vulnerable to abuse and neglect, and yet vigilant and ever-loving. May we desire to imitate the mystery we partake of and attempt to make frequent Communion a marriage goal. May your Eucharistic heart remind us that we remain in our vows not simply for the sake of the other, but out of love for you. Might we aspire to make frequent visits to you in the tabernacle, to keep you company when you are all alone. Help us to shake off our indifference to your presence among us and guard our hearts in your love.

OR—

Meditation

Today's celebration of the Eucharist is, in part, a celebration of marriage: the marriage between God and man in the person of Jesus Christ. True God and true man, the Lord's own personhood perfects the covenant God once established with his Chosen People (the Jews) and extends it to the entire world for those who believe in his name. Architecturally, the Church has honored this nuptiality with the use of a *baldacchino* or wedding canopy over the altar. The most prominent of its kind adorns the high altar at St. Peter's Basilica in Rome. On the altar, humanity and divinity are wed together in the sacrament of the most holy Eucharist, the new and everlasting covenant. This indicates how God sees his people redeemed by the Lord's Blood: in nuptial terms. The Father pursues us until we are possessed by him in love. And to nourish us along the journey, he feeds us with the Son's Body and Blood so that we might imitate the mystery we celebrate—being broken and spent for one another. Hence, marriage is not some ancillary reality in God's eyes—it is central to the drama of salvation. Couples have a particular responsibility to bear this out in the world by their spousal love—reminding the world how God loves us.

Question(s) / Prayer

Father, help us to see and understand our marriage as a participation in the grand work of salvation that your Son won for us at Calvary. Might we better understand that our vocation is not just about us. Rather, it is a witness to the love you have for your people, understood in nuptial and covenantal terms. May we imitate your fidelity, unwavering pursuit of your beloved, and self-sacrificing love manifested in Jesus' redemptive work at Calvary.

SOLEMNITY OF THE MOST SACRED HEART OF JESUS—FRIDAY AFTER THE MOST HOLY BODY AND BLOOD

GOSPEL: MATTHEW 11:25-30 (YEAR A) / JOHN 19:31-37 (YEAR B) / LUKE 15:3-7 (YEAR C)

Meditation

Jesus describes his heart as being meek and humble. Humility, in principle, is easy enough to understand. The Latin word *humilitas* takes its root from the word *humus*, which means "dirt." (*Humus* should not be confused with *hummus*, which is a delicious Middle Eastern dipping paste.) Perhaps this is why we describe humble persons as "grounded." Meekness, however, is less well understood. Meekness is the virtue of self-control or self-possession. In popular parlance, it is equated with timidity, but this is not a Biblical understanding of the word. Meek persons are neither too emotionally hot or cold, high or low. Instead, they are level-headed, balanced, self-controlled, and not given to overly strong emotions. They tend to be very agreeable persons with whom to live, as they are not easily given to mood swings or worse—unabated anger. Both virtues (meekness and humility) are needed for any marriage to thrive. They are virtues that tend to assist spouses to forgive easily and ask for forgiveness promptly. These virtues always cultivate respect for the other person, never giving in to arrogance or presumption. Undoubtedly, they are indispensable for any healthy and holy marriage.

Question(s) / Prayer

Lord, help us to imitate your Sacred Heart, especially through the two virtues that you used to describe your heart, which beats out of love, mercy, and compassion for us. Might we take seriously the cultivation of both humility and meekness, especially if we have deficits in these areas, which make us difficult to love. Help us to understand that every day is another opportunity to practice humility by accepting humiliations gracefully (and not resentfully), and to exercise the self-control needed to prosper in our marriage. May proper discernment help us to see that self-control does not mean neglecting to speak up when we must, but doing so with charity and mercy.

FEAST OF THE TRANSFIGURATION OF THE LORD—AUGUST 6

GOSPEL: MATTHEW 17:1-9 (YEAR A) / MARK 9:2-10 (YEAR B) / LUKE 9:28B-36 (YEAR C)

Meditation

The Transfiguration constitutes the literary pivot of the synoptic Gospels. In Matthew, Mark, and Luke, this event marks the final turn that Jesus makes from Galilee in the north, south in direction but up in elevation towards the dramatic events of Holy Week in Jerusalem. Jesus is revealed between Moses and Elijah, indicating that he is the fulfillment of the Law and the Prophets.

In the visible created order, the human person is uniquely capable of imagining the infinite. And yet we face the daily reality of the finite. We exist in this tension between the finitude of our lives and our capacity to long for the infinite, which is ultimately God. The Transfiguration addresses the complexity of our predicament. Peter, James, and John are described as being "very much afraid" (Mt 17:6) or "terrified" (Mk 9:6) or "frightened" (Lk 9:34) at the sight of the Transfigured Lord, depending on what version of the narrative you read. Jesus shows them a glimpse of Easter glory that is intended to steel their resolve after the terror about the impending Crucifixion. The climax of the story is already revealed: the Cross will not ultimately be a cause of shame because death will not have the final word and Jesus will be vindicated in the Resurrection—paving our path to the same.

Peter's actions, more than his words, tell the true story about this tension between the finite and the infinite. Peter's instant reaction is to build tents or booths in honor of Jesus, Moses, and Elijah. He's ready to get busy. And yet we know that deep interior conversion doesn't start or even end with busyness. Rather, it's rooted in contemplation of the Holy Face in all of its resplendent glory. It requires listening and not speaking and being conformed to the Lord rather than conforming him to our established patterns of thought and behavior.

Question(s) / Prayer

Lord, we pray that you allow the mystery of the glory of the Transfiguration to console, inspire, challenge, and move us to contemplate how it is only the infinite—God—that can enact the grace of interior conversion necessary to satiate our deepest longings for salvation and for transformation into the saints the Father intends us to be.

FEAST OF THE EXALTATION OF THE HOLY CROSS—SEPTEMBER 14

GOSPEL: JOHN 3:13-17

Meditation

The Cross remains among the central mysteries of Christian faith. It represents the great paradox of glory in suffering, life through death, and love born out of hatred. Christ's one and definitive atoning sacrifice on the tree of the Cross reverses the ancient curse wrought by Adam and Eve's disobedient act of eating of the tree in the Garden of Eden. The Cross is the foundation of every vocation, including marriage. In many Eastern European countries, married couples pronounce their vows while jointly clasping a cross—a cross which will hang in their new home. This is to remind the couple of their need to die to their individual preferences in favor of the common good of the marriage and children. Every follower of the Lord is invited into the great theo-drama of participating in the Cross of Christ by their lives of faith. And as the great antidote to selfishness, pride, arrogance, and materialism, the Cross teaches self-sacrifice, humility, mildness, and a detachment from worldliness. Paradoxically, Christ is the happiest of men as he hangs on the Cross—not because he is not suffering, but because he is doing the will of the Father. This is the pattern and model for all discipleship.

Question(s) / Prayer

Lord, help us to enter more fully into the mystery of the Cross in our lives. Make us grateful for the virtues the Cross teaches us. Help us to embrace the crosses marriage presents each of us with daily. May we not shy away from the Cross, but accept it willingly and joyfully, knowing that by our lives of faith we accomplish your will by participating in your ultimate act of love for us.

SOLEMNITY OF OUR LORD JESUS CHRIST, KING OF THE UNIVERSE—THE LAST SUNDAY OF THE LITURGICAL YEAR

GOSPEL: MATTHEW 25:31-46 (YEAR A) / JOHN 18:33B-37 (YEAR B) / LUKE 23:35-43 (YEAR C)

Meditation

Europe was in flames. Attila the Hun was sweeping through a collapsing Roman Empire—bringing death, ruin, and terror wherever he went. The Empire was too weak to defend itself. The end seemed near. St. Martin of Tours wrote that the Antichrist had been born. St. Augustine wrote *The City of God* to calm fears in light of the collapse of civilization, assuring people of God's constant concern. The stage was set for Christ to return. Pope St. Leo the Great went unarmed to meet Attila at the town of Peschiera. The year was 452. What was said will never be known. What is known is that the Hun was turned back by the priest. Leo had revealed to Attila a vision of the Last Judgement. Attila the Hun, who feared no mortal, learned the fear of God. Attila died. Leo died. And the world continued.

Europe was in flames—flames set not by Huns and Mongols, but by Vikings to the north, Muslims to the south, and Magyars to the east. Plagues decimated the populations of many villages. Charlemagne, who had held Europe together, was long dead and the throne was usurped by Otto the Saxon and powerful French barons who brushed aside the weak Louis IV. The year was 963. As the year 1000 approached, the general feeling was that Christ would return for the Last Judgement. Pope Sylvester II had a speech prepared to welcome the Lord before the business of Judgement began. The mystic Abbot Adso of Montier-en-Der wrote his frightening "Letter on the Origin and Time of the Antichrist." Otto the Saxon died. Adso of Montier-en-Der died. Sylvester II died. And the world continued.

Europe was in flames. The late Middle Ages and early Renaissance had been periods of progress in the arts and sciences, but also a time of tremendous fracturing in Europe, a time of many wars to mark off the boundaries of modern European countries as they broke from the old empires. The Church was blessed with great saints: Blessed John Duns Scotus, SS. Thomas More and John Fisher, St. Angela Merici and St. Catherine of Siena. The Church enjoyed the work of great artists like Michelangelo, Rafael, and Palestrina. She was also plagued by immoral popes and bishops. There was a great division in the Church with three men claiming to be pope at the same time. The real popes had moved from Italy to Avignon, France, and then back again after about eighty years. The Black Death stalked the major cities of Europe, and civilization was again threatened by the Muslims who wanted a hostile takeover. The end of the world seemed very near, for Europe was teetering on the brink of political disaster and the Church was rotting at every level. The Dominican Friar Girolamo Savonarola preached a need for repentance and reform because the justice of God would be swift and severe. The immoral popes died. The Muslims were beaten back at the battle of Lepanto. Savonarola was burned at the stake. And the world continued ... except for them.

Europe was in flames. The Allies were combating Germany, Austria-Hungary, Turkey, and Bulgaria. The legacy of World War I was widespread atheism across Europe, a loss of faith in Christ and the Church. Atheistic communism began to be a state-sponsored ideology. The destruction of World War I had surpassed the combined loss of all previous wars. Pope Pius XI excommunicated all Catholics who were members of the Communist Party. A voice from shepherd children in the countryside of Fatima, Portugal, said that repentance and conversion were essential. Russia must be converted, lest it be the Antichrist. The end of the world seemed near. Joseph Stalin died. The Soviet Union died. Communism died. And the world continues ... and so do the flames.

In all ages except our own, the return of Jesus at the Final Judgement has been the object of prayer and the hope of believers. Somehow, in this age, possibly because of the many movies that glamorize evil, we now want to run and hide from God, like the freshly fallen Adam in the Garden of Eden. But the Church—proclaiming the Gospel of her Spouse—says that the Gospel doesn't have to be a message that stifles joy. In fact, the Gospel should cause joy. "Your Kingdom come" (Mt 6:10) is the prayer given to us by Christ Himself. There will be wars and plagues and persecutions. There always have been. There still are. I would imagine that there will be for a long time to come. The prophets of the apocalypse come around not every five hundred years—but they're always with us.

We likely have known people who lived through the polio epidemic, World War II, and the Nazi Holocaust. And who can forget the chaos wrought by the global pandemic of 2019-2021? At this moment, we are all living through the plague of substance abuse, the war against terrorism, and the holocaust of the unborn, which has now quadrupled the number of casualties of the Nazi holocaust. The twentieth century was the bloodiest of all centuries. There are signs of doom, and there are good reasons to rush to confession. Undeniable. Many at this moment live not in a political apocalypse, but a personal apocalypse of sin, moral compromise, sickness, divorce, or loneliness, or something else that breaks our heart. We are invited today to open ourselves to the one we love—the one we hear in the first reading, who is the ever-watchful and ever-protecting shepherd of his people, his beloved Church. He is the one who promises to reward our earthly fidelity with an eternal life with him, a life of unimaginable fulfillment and peace: "Come, you who are blessed by my Father. Inherit the kingdom prepared for you from the foundation of the world" (Mt 25:34).

In the face of all signs of despair and distrust in our own day and city, in spite of all temptations to write off estranged family members or friends, through all our heartache and the illnesses we may suffer, let us take very much to heart Jesus' words today. May our prayers bring hope and deep peace to those who need them. May we derive a sense of justice and sacrifice from our discipleship that makes us sensitive and mature. May we *always* trust Jesus the Lord despite so many signs of hopelessness and despair. May the Lord always hold us near his Sacred Heart and may the Blessed Virgin Mary, whose own heart was pierced with the lance of sorrow, teach us peace and serenity in an uncertain world.

Question(s) / Prayer

Is the Lord the true king of our lives? If not, what are we prepared to do in order to make that a reality?

SOLEMNITIES AND FEAST DAYS OF SAINTS

SOLEMNITY OF MARY, THE HOLY MOTHER OF GOD—JANUARY 1

GOSPEL: LUKE 2:16-21

Meditation

Many scholars agree that our Lady was probably the source material for many of the infancy narratives in Luke's Gospel, since the details could only have been known by an eyewitness to the events themselves. And early in Luke's Gospel, we learn about our Lady's interior life. Luke writes that "Mary kept all these things, reflecting on them in her heart" (Lk 2:19). This detail indicates that Mary lived an active life (keeping house and raising the Lord in Nazareth) with a contemplative spirit. Nothing about our Lord or the Father's designs of divine providence escaped her. She was given the gift not of memory and retention, but of spiritual insight into what the events occurring around her meant. She was able to perceive and absorb how God was using her vocation to work out his grand designs of salvation for the world. This is a contemplative spirit that we should all pray for—the capacity to see things as they truly are, and from the viewpoint of the Holy Trinity. In our busyness, we are prone to overlook so many details and seemingly small events that are God's subtle way of working out his plan for us. We can miss signs that he is giving us to guide us to our heavenly homeland. Every believer should pray to cultivate a deep Marian spirit that reflects upon God's activity with a heart that is pure and full of love.

Question(s) / Prayer

Do we take time to keep and reflect upon what God is doing in our lives? Are we too busy with so many needless things, so that we miss the subtle signs he wants to give us? Do we have pure hearts that see God and all that he wishes for us? Do we create the interior silence necessary to make room for the Lord—the interior silence that allows us to breathe in the Holy Spirit and breathe out the anxieties of life that distract us from our vocation to be saints?

FEAST OF THE CONVERSION OF ST. PAUL, APOSTLE—JANUARY 25

GOSPEL: MARK 16:15-18

Meditation

In his lifetime, St. Paul took to heart today's admonition to go into the whole world and proclaim the Gospel to every creature. His indefatigable zeal for souls and his boundless energy lit aflame large portions of the Mediterranean world and galvanized Rome as the seat of the Church, which then Christianized Western civilization. In St. Paul, God had the quintessential messenger: a former Pharisee steeped in Judaism, but also well-versed in Greco-Roman languages and philosophy owing to his Roman citizenship and education. Imagine all that he accomplished in spite of the fact that he did not have the advantages of modern transportation or communication! He is truly one of the most remarkable saints in the history of the Church and rightly referred to as a super Apostle. Led by the Holy Spirit, he overcame extreme hardships to preach the Gospel, save souls, and establish early Christian communities. We are all the beneficiaries of this Apostle's incredible spirit and grace-filled ministry. St. Paul's faith was based on a personal encounter with the Lord on the road to Damascus. St. Paul wasn't simply won over by the philosophical and theological arguments of Christianity. In fact, most of those were still in their nascent forms! Instead, Paul was enraptured by the personal meeting he had with the Lord, which forever changed the course of his life.

Question(s) / Prayer

Lord, imbue us with your Holy Spirit so that we are lit aflame with zeal for the souls we encounter in our families, our workplaces, and our schools, and within our circles of friends and acquaintances. May we never cite our lack of resources as an excuse for not evangelizing those who have yet to encounter you personally. May we be willing to give convincing and heart-felt testimony about our friendship with you and those Damascus moments we experience. May our testimony be based less on arguments for the Catholic faith and based more on our experience of your mercy and love. Like St. Paul, may we learn to harness all of our resources for your greater glory and the salvation of souls.

FEAST OF THE CHAIR OF ST. PETER THE APOSTLE—FEBRUARY 22

GOSPEL: MATTHEW 16:13-19

Meditation

The symbolism of the chair is ancient in Western civilization as a sign of teaching authority. For instance, the "county seat" is the typical office of the magistrate (from the Latin, *magister*, or teacher). The term "Holy See" (the Vatican) is the old English term meaning "Holy Seat." Prominent professors vie for endowed "chairs" at universities. Similarly, musicians compete to be in the "first chair." A diocesan bishop's church is called a cathedral, from the Latin *cathedra* or seat. Today's feast celebrates the teaching office of the Petrine ministry, exercised by the pope. It reminds us that the Church is the custodian, not the inventor, of the sacred Deposit of Faith, handed down by Christ to the Apostles through two millennia of Christian history. The liberating truth of the Gospel inspired the European continent to produce Western civilization and all of its advances in science, literature, art, music, language, diplomacy, education, discovery, and agriculture. Hence, Christianity isn't simply a philosophical or theological tradition—its saving truth is a worldview that enshrines serious a priori commitments about human dignity and the salvation of the human race through Christ's redeeming sacrifice on the Cross. And everything that Europe has produced over the centuries points to one stark reality: All roads lead to Rome. And at the heart of that Roman culture stands Holy Mother Church—nurturing her children to everlasting life.

Question(s) / Prayer

Lord, help us to rediscover the role our marriage and family should play in the life of the Church. Might we appreciate that it is through the domestic church (the home) that children learn about the Christian roots of Western civilization and its impact on world history. Help us to see that we have been given the richest of patrimonies and that it is our privilege and duty to hand it on to future generations, sensing the weight of our history and tradition. Whenever our youth are tempted to abandon the Faith, help us to help them see what they are giving up!

SOLEMNITY OF ST. JOSEPH, SPOUSE OF THE BLESSED VIRGIN—MARCH 19

GOSPEL: MATTHEW 1:16, 18-21, 24A OR LUKE 2:41-51A

Meditation

The silence of St. Joseph throughout the infancy and childhood narratives of the Lord speaks volumes. Nowhere do we find Joseph protesting or complaining about the various commands he is given by the Father, primarily in dreams. His purity of heart allows him to absorb and assimilate whatever God wants of him, and he readily puts forth his best effort in trust. He is not a man of means, but what he has, he surrenders to God to be used for his purposes and not his own. He is never self-seeking in his endeavors but maintains a posture of complete docility and generosity. He does not keep score or count the cost when it comes to giving, and he exudes an aura of strength and authority, even if he has no speaking role. Foster father to the Son of God and chaste spouse of the Queen of Heaven and Earth, Joseph knows his rightful place in the economy of salvation. His virtues motivated St. John XXIII to name him Patron of the Universal Church. We ought to go to St. Joseph with trust. Husbands should maintain a strong devotion to him and be consecrated to one of the most revered saints in the Church's history, guardian of the Redeemer and our Lady.

Question(s) / Prayer

Heavenly Father, whenever we are tempted to complain or protest against you because your plans and ours don't coalesce, may we turn to St. Joseph and learn from his docility and generosity. May our lack of resources (temporal and spiritual) never dissuade us from accomplishing what you have given us to do for your greater glory and the salvation of our souls and those entrusted to our care. Help us to cultivate St. Joseph's virtue of silence, which creates the space necessary for us to hear your voice and not merely our own.

SOLEMNITY OF THE ANNUNCIATION OF THE LORD—MARCH 25

GOSPEL: LUKE 1:26-38

Meditation

The celebration of this solemnity takes place precisely nine months prior to Christmas, respectful of the typical gestation period for babies. March 25 as a date on the calendar is therefore *relative* to another milestone date: Christmas. This relativity follows the pattern of the Blessed Mother: Her role in salvation history is always *relative* to Christ, her son and our Lord. Her life's work finds its reference in her son. The Lord's first and most perfect disciple reminds us that our lives, too, ought to find Christ as their reference point. We know our true selves only in light of knowing Christ, for it is the Lord who reveals to us who we are (sinners) and who we can become (saints)!

Our Lady's posture at the Annunciation establishes our pattern for discipleship: docile, humble, simple, pure, and obedient. It is said that Mary conceived the Lord in her heart before she conceived him in her body. And so it should be with us—always demonstrating good works animated by interior conversion and conviction.

Furthermore, genuine discipleship is much more than a private experience—it is always outward in its mission. Notice that soon after this event, our Lady proceeds *in haste* to visit St. Elizabeth, already six months pregnant with St. John the Baptist. Not content with relishing her role as the Mother of God, she is *in via* (on the way).

Question(s) / Prayer

Lord, help us to imitate the virtues of our Lady! When we are tempted to selfishness and pride, may she teach us generosity and humility. When we are tempted to autonomy and self-reliance, may she teach us filial dependence and trust in you. When we are tempted to be willful, may she teach us docility. And when we are tempted to lust, may she teach us purity and chastity.

O Mary, conceived without sin, pray for us who have recourse to thee!

FEAST OF ST. MARK, EVANGELIST—APRIL 25

GOSPEL: MARK 16:15-20

Meditation

One of the most overlooked yet remarkable lines in the Gospel according to St. Mark is the opening line, "The Gospel of Jesus Christ, the Son of God." Moderns may not appreciate it, but those were fighting words. Keep in mind that it's quite likely that Mark wrote this line soon after witnessing the death of St. Peter by crucifixion upside down in the emperor Nero's circus (arena) on the Vatican Hill across the Tiber from downtown Rome. The word "Gospel" (or *evangelion* in Greek) meant a proclamation of great importance (usually, a military victory) and the title "Son of God" was reserved for the emperor. So what Mark is saying is that Jesus Christ is the true emperor who has conquered sin and eternal death, as witnessed to (*martyrein* is the Greek verb meaning "witness to") by St. Peter's death. He who had denied Christ thrice had conquered his failure by giving the ultimate witness to the Lord, the true emperor of the universe.

Question(s) / Prayer

Lord, grant us the grace to witness to you in the daily events of our lives. May we never hesitate to proclaim you as the Lord of our lives and the person to whom we owe ultimate loyalty. When we are difficult to love, help us to remember that we promised to love one another out of love for you, the source of all love. May you reign supreme in our hearts and may the manner of our lives reflect your kingship of charity and interior freedom.

OPTIONAL MEMORIAL OF ST. JOSEPH THE WORKER—MAY 1

GOSPEL: MATTHEW 13:54-58

Meditation

The question in today's gospel passage, "Is he not the carpenter's son?" (Mt 13:55) was not a straightforward query put forward by the Lord's fellow Nazarenes. It had a derogatory tone, since carpenters were not considered high-status workers. But the Lord was never embarrassed to be known as a carpenter's son. It was in St. Joseph's workshop that the Lord learned the Psalms (which Jewish men often repeated as they worked). With every stroke of the hammer, it is noteworthy that the Lord knew of that ultimate meeting he would have with wood at Calvary. St. Joseph taught the Lord (in his humanity) the meaning of an honest day's work and the importance work has for preserving human dignity (especially in the male instinct to want to provide for a family). Historically, this feast was included in the liturgical calendar as a Catholic response to May Day celebrations sponsored by Marxists, Socialists, and Communists, all of whom make work an end and not a means to salvation. St. Joseph teaches the Church and the world that work is an imitation of the Father's creative instinct (the Book of Genesis begins with the story of the work of creation) and that the Sabbath rest is also needed to re-create and reorient one's life back to God.

Question(s) / Prayer

What role does work play in our marriage and family? Does it occupy its proper place, always secondary to our marriage and family life? Or does it dominate and dictate the rhythm of our lives? Do we make compromises with work since more income can provide a lifestyle we prefer? Is work simply a means to the great end we all seek (salvation), or is it a demi-god that makes unreasonable demands on us that we can never satisfy?

FEAST OF SS. PHILIP AND JAMES, APOSTLES—MAY 3

GOSPEL: JOHN 14:6-14

Meditation

The Apostles, including our feast day saints, were slow to understand that Jesus truly is the Son of God. And who can blame them? Raised in Judaism, the concept of God coming so close to the human family so as to take upon himself human nature was radically novel. For the Apostles to believe that whoever saw Jesus was seeing the Father was a major leap of faith! And while these realities seem commonplace to us two millennia after they were revealed, the Apostles were seeing them for the first time. But it was not enough for the Lord to manifest himself in this unique way—he wanted (and wants) his disciples to know that those who believe in him will do his works. There's a real connection the Lord wants to have with us—one that transcends mere forensic appreciation for his sonship to the Father. Jesus desires much more—that his disciples become united to him in everything. Jesus' vision for our discipleship defies the all-too-common tendency we have to keep the Lord at a distance, where he is safe and manageable for us.

Question(s) / Prayer

Lord, whenever we are tempted to give in to the all-too-common tendency we have to keep you at a distance, where you are safe and manageable for us, help us to understand that you desire to dwell in and among us. This first happens through Baptism, is nourished in the Eucharist, is renewed by each sacramental confession, and finds a specific expression in marriage. Grant us, we pray, the courage to enter deeply into the communion you desire for us—one that demands a total giving of ourselves to you and each other.

FEAST OF ST. MATTHIAS, APOSTLE—MAY 14

GOSPEL: JOHN 15:9-17

Meditation

The Lord's invitation to friendship has a distinctive flavor: Jesus' invitation to friendship connotes a closeness and intimacy, but it does not make us his equals. This is why the Lord can say, "You are my friends if you do what I command you" (Jn 15:14). This is not a demand any of us can make of our friends in ordinary circumstances. But the statement implies that we are the Lord's friends if *and only if* we do what he commands us. In other words, disobedience is tantamount to a betrayal of friendship. Remarkably, the Lord does not simply command us to obey him. He goes the full distance—to lay down his life for us, in the ultimate act of love any friend can offer. The friends of the Lord are thus commanded to love as he loves—by laying down their lives for one another. Unfortunately, many marriages falter and fail because the spirit of Jesus—to live a life of self-sacrifice—wanes in the relationship. When couples start counting the cost or keeping score, trouble surely lurks. When couples begin to say to one another, "It's my turn now. You had your way last time," the once noble aspiration to die to self in order to live for the other has lost its luster. While the Lord did not direct these verses to married persons per se, they contain riches worth contemplating and actualizing in any God-fearing marriage.

Question(s) / Prayer

Lord, help us to love as you love. Help us to relish being your friends and all that that relationship entails. Thank you for considering us your friends and not merely your slaves. Give us the confidence that the Father chose us for one another, just as he chooses us individually to live in communion with him. Grant us the insight to understand the freedom that comes with obedience to the will of the Father. May we cooperate with the graces you provide to help us avoid giving in to our willfulness and the illusion of autonomy.

FEAST OF THE VISITATION OF THE BLESSED VIRGIN MARY—MAY 31

GOSPEL: LUKE 1:39-56

Meditation

The opening line of today's gospel passage often gets overlooked. Luke writes, "Mary set out and traveled to the hill country in haste..." (Lk 1:39). It's worth considering the context. Our Lady has just accepted the Father's proposal to be the Mother of God. It would have been understandable if travel to the hill country (about ninety miles south) was the last thing on her mind. But our Lady's love for Elizabeth cannot be contained. She not only made an arduous journey through muddy roads in the spring, she did so in haste! Love moves persons to act with urgency and purpose! Our Lady is never lethargic and passive in her love. Rather, her love is marked with alacrity and determination. It is a love that does not rest until it possesses the object desired. And Mary loves her spiritual children with the same spirit! She so desires to be an integral part of a couple's marriage, given that she herself was a married woman and mother. But our Lady will never impose herself where she is not welcome. She never forces her way in—always respectful of the free will of her children. And even when we are distant from her, she always intercedes on our behalf, asking for graces that we often don't even realize we need or know to ask for.

Question(s) / Prayer

Lord, grant us the spirit of urgency that our Lady showed in coming to Elizabeth's home. Like Elizabeth, may we always rejoice when our Lady is near and like St. John the Baptist, may we recognize the Lord's presence even when it is not obvious to us. Help us to love one another with alacrity and purpose—never to become passive or lethargic in our love for our spouse. Grace us with the peace that comes with having our Lady's presence in our marriage, since she is the surest path to you.

SOLEMNITY OF THE NATIVITY OF JOHN THE BAPTIST—JUNE 24

GOSPEL: LUKE 1:5-17 (VIGIL), LUKE 1:57-66,80

Meditation

It seems that everything about John the Baptist was exceptional: being born to elderly parents; his father (Zechariah) being cast mute prior to John's birth; the events of the Visitation and his fetal awareness that the Lord was near; the choice of his name; John's eccentric diet and ministry in the desert of Judea; his insistence that he was not the Christ in spite of popular acclaim; his remarkable courage in witnessing to the sanctity of marriage in the face of Herod's adultery. But there is one dimension of John the Baptist's life that is often overlooked: his eschewing of his rightful place to serve as a priest in the Temple. In Judaism, priesthood was conferred by hereditary inheritance among the members of the tribe of Levi (see Deuteronomy 18). It would have been expected for Zechariah, himself a priest, to pass along this mantle to his exceptional son. But as we know, this did not happen. Instead, John embarked on preaching to prepare the Lord's arrival. Unsurprisingly, this foregoing of what would have been a very comfortable and prestigious lifestyle (as a Temple priest), remains consistent with John's constant surpassing of human expectations and conventions.

Question(s) / Prayer

Heavenly Father, help us to be open to the surprises that you wish to confer upon us in marriage—surprises that go against or beyond conventional thinking about marriage and family. Perhaps it means having more children. Perhaps it means finding a way to live off of one primary income so that mom can stay home and raise the children. Perhaps it means taking less expensive vacations in favor of donating money to the poor. Perhaps it means eschewing the temptation to keep up with our peers in the way of houses, cars, trips, lifestyle. Might the example of St. John the Baptist give us courage to be exceptional in your eyes.

SOLEMNITY OF SS. PETER AND PAUL, APOSTLES—JUNE 29

GOSPEL: MATTHEW 16:13-19 (MASS DURING THE DAY)

Meditation

There are two answers to the question Jesus puts to the disciples in today's Gospel: "Who do you say that I am?" (Mt 16:15). First, Peter's confession of faith renders the objective answer—Jesus is the Christ! Its objectivity is confirmed by the Lord's statement that Peter's answer was given to him by the Father (and not flesh and blood). In other words, in a moment of infused knowledge, the Father grants Peter true insight into Jesus' true identity for the benefit of the others. Peter's answer isn't merely his opinion—he is speaking on behalf of the Father to give us the truth. Second, there is another dimension of answering the same question—the subjective answer. In other words, each individual follower or would-be follower of Jesus needs to align the objective answer given by Peter with the subjective answer to the question, "Who is Jesus for me?" Problems arise when we exalt the subjective answer over the objective answer, thus creating a Jesus that caters to subjective desires and needs. The challenge of discipleship is to venerate the objective answer and to align one's life (subjectively) with it.

Question(s) / Prayer

Lord, help us to align our subjective perceptions with the objective truth that Peter gives us in today's Gospel. Might we trust that this re-orientation of our lives will provide the interior freedom that we all desire, knowing that we are not our own god, but your servants in faith, hope, and love. Help us to place you, and not our own egos, at the center of our lives and our marriage. May we become resolute in doing your will and not merely our own. And may we be eager to place our resources at your feet so that we can join Peter in acknowledging that you are truly the Son of God.

FEAST OF ST. THOMAS, APOSTLE—JULY 3

GOSPEL: JOHN 20:24-29

Meditation

The healing of Thomas's unbelief by his experience of the resurrected Lord was thorough and complete. Not only did Thomas witness physical evidence of Jesus' resurrected body, which bears the marks of the Passion but feels no pain—Thomas also discovered that the Lord could hear him even though he was not physically present when Thomas claimed unbelief. When Jesus appears, the Lord anticipates Thomas's rejection of the claims of the other Apostles. Thomas did not bother to ask the Lord how he knew what he had said in his lack of faith. It is also important to note that all of this was predicated not only on the facts surrounding the Lord's resurrection. It was also predicated on the eyewitness testimony of the Apostles, who told Thomas about what they had experienced in their encounter with the risen Lord. This has been the story of the Church and all of her sons and daughters through twenty centuries of Christian history. The Faith has been passed down from generation to generation on the basis of the testimony of our forefathers in the Church. But for many, many decades now, the witness of successive generations of believers has faded. Once very religious families have fallen into mass apostasy or indifference over the generations. How few persons now can truly say about Jesus, "My Lord and my God"? This places immense responsibilities on parents to pass on the Faith to their children with credibility, gravitas, and joy.

Question(s) / Prayer

Are we confident that the Faith will live on in our family, at least in our children and among the next generation we can influence? Do we take seriously the witness of the Apostles and especially of the martyrs, who made the ultimate sacrifice so that we might hear the Gospel and be saved? Are we convinced that belief in Christ is necessary for salvation, or do we simply relegate our treasured Catholic faith to the status of just one of many paths to eternal life?

FEAST OF ST. MARY MAGDALENE—JULY 22

GOSPEL: JOHN 20:1-2, 11-18

Meditation

It's easy to overlook a small but significant detail about the appearance of Jesus as a gardener. The Fathers of the Church recognized a simple truth about this detail: Jesus appeared as a gardener because gardeners have important work to accomplish each spring—to restore order to a disordered garden. Disorder entered the world in the Garden of Eden. Order was restored in the Garden of the Tomb. Prior to meeting the Lord, Mary Magdalene had lived a disordered life. Jesus brought order, light, and peace to her life. But he did not do this in a merely superficial way, as if to give her self-help guidance. Rather, the Lord healed her at her core—in her soul. He opened for her a new path to life. He saw her true self and instead of rejecting or condemning her, the Lord restored her dignity. When most would have dismissed her, the Lord saw great possibilities. How indebted she must have felt to him for saving her life.

Question (s) / Prayer

Are we resolved to allow Jesus to restore order in our individual lives and in our marriage? Do we perceive those areas that are not quite right with the Lord and need reorganization and healing? Do we have that same sense of indebtedness to the Lord for having saved us? Do we ask Jesus to help heal our individual and collective wounds?

FEAST OF ST. JAMES THE GREAT, APOSTLE—JULY 25

GOSPEL: MATTHEW 20:20-28

Meditation

Scholars agree that one of the marks of the authenticity of the Gospels is the inclusion of stories like the one depicted in today's Gospel. It shows a very unflattering picture of two of the Lord's closest associates. To add insult to injury, these grown men allow their mother to speak on their behalf! Perhaps the logic of the Cross hadn't quite made enough of an impression on James and John. Jesus has just finished predicting the type of death he was to endure in Jerusalem. All that the Sons of Thunder can do is to seek places at our Lord's right and left in his Kingdom! Like many of their peers, James and John may have thought that our Lord's kingdom would be an earthly, political one. Eventually they would see how foolish their request was, given that the Lord had come to do much more—he came to save the human race from sin and eternal death. In other words, James and John are asking for the wrong thing! Over time, James and John will learn how much greater Jesus' vision and horizon are. This, too, is a challenge for married couples. It takes spiritual maturity to broaden the horizon of what marriage can mean to spouses. For some, it's about raising a family and having life companionship. For others, marriage is about experiencing a humanly fulfilling relationship. But for couples married in Christ, it's that and much more—it's about becoming saints in the world and getting to heaven!

Question(s) / Prayer

Lord, when we are tempted to categorize you in one form or another or define you according to what we expect from you, help us to remember this scene in the Gospel. Help us to appreciate our married vocation as a Cross whose burden is light. Help us to integrate the logic of the Cross into the trials and tribulations that we endure in our vocation. They are the means by which we can grow closer to you and one another. Broaden the horizon of our marriage so we can see what this project is really all about—that a sacramental marriage is about sanctity and sainthood, not simply the natural goods that marriage entails (a life-long bond that is faithful and open to life). Help us to see that a marriage in Christ transcends mere human categories and is the ordinary way in which we will be saved, if we are disposed to taking up our Cross and following you always. Lord, we know that it's easy for anyone to ask you for the wrong things—things that won't really matter in the end. May St. James intercede for us to ask for those things that we really need to get to heaven.

FEAST OF ST. LAWRENCE, DEACON AND MARTYR—AUGUST 10

GOSPEL: JOHN 12:24-26

Meditation

Today's gospel passage is appropriate any time a martyr's feast day is celebrated. After all, martyrs make the ultimate sacrifice and pay the highest price out of love for Christ and zeal for souls. The paradox of the Cross looms large: It is in dying to oneself that the human person discovers the depths of love. Sacrifice is usually difficult and irksome. Only love can make it easy, and perfect love can make it a joy. We are willing to give in proportion as we love. And when love is perfect, sacrifice is complete. But the sacrifice ought not to be understood apart from joy and even mirth. St. Lawrence, above all the martyrs, was alleged to have had a sense of humor about his torturous death—he exhorted his executioners to turn him over ("I'm done on this side") on the gridiron upon which he was being burnt alive! This holy detachment contains a lesson for all: When love informs sacrifice, it can be difficult and yet fulfilling. Married persons are perfectly positioned to experience this frequently and deeply. There ought to be a joy that accompanies willingly sacrificing for one's beloved. It's the type of sacrifice that does not count the cost or expect thanks or recognition. For this type of spouse, loving is its own reward.

Question(s) / Prayer

Are we as willing to sacrifice for each other, as we are for our children? Do we delight in loving as its own reward, or are we busy keeping score and counting the cost? Do we harbor resentments toward our spouse because we feel as if we've been asked to give up too much? Do we look to the martyrs, not with a victim/martyr complex, but with a heart inspired by their willingness to love others out of love for Christ?

SOLEMNITY OF THE ASSUMPTION OF THE BLESSED VIRGIN MARY—AUGUST 15

GOSPEL: LUKE 1:39-56

Meditation

The dogma of the Assumption of the Blessed Virgin Mary is the logical conclusion of the dogma of the Immaculate Conception. Recall that having been conceived without Original Sin, our Lady was not subject to the corrupting powers of death. While her life on earth came to an end, she never experienced death as the separation of body and soul. Rather, her body and soul—preserved from the stain of Original Sin—were assumed into heaven. And all of this is true thanks to her privileged role as the Mother of God (the first of the Marian dogmas), passing on perfect humanity to the Lord—the Son of God and Son of Mary. Solemnities like today's celebration cause us to take pause and marvel at what God has done for us through our Lady! God's love for us is so immense that he placed before us individuals such as the Blessed Virgin Mary to mediate the mysteries of salvation. This awareness was not lost on either St. Elizabeth or John the Baptist, featured prominently in today's Gospel. Both of them had an intimate and deep awareness of our Lady and our Lord's presence among them and what their lives on earth would mean for the salvation of the world.

Question(s) / Prayer

O Mary, conceived without sin, pray for us who have recourse to thee!

Queen of all Saints, pray for us!
Queen conceived without Original Sin, pray for us!
Queen assumed into heaven, pray for us!
Queen of families, pray for us!
Queen of peace. pray for us!

FEAST OF ST. BARTHOLOMEW, APOSTLE—AUGUST 24

GOSPEL: JOHN 1:45-51

Meditation

St. Bartholomew (a.k.a. St. Nathanael) was praised by the Lord for having "no duplicity" (Jn 1:47). The term is often conflated with having "no guile." In this great Apostle-saint, the Lord found a sincere and genuine individual—the type of person one would describe as "What you see is what you get." Such persons enjoy an integrated personality. Hence, they avoid hypocrisy and the two-facedness that can drive would-be followers of the Lord far away. Recall that the Lord was often very critical of the Pharisees and other religious elites precisely because of their hypocrisy. They would make grandiose gestures of religiosity while living dissolute lives in private. Even now, this type of wholeness can be threatening to those who struggle with duplicity and moral compromise. The uncomplicated manner of "Nathanaels" can make those who struggle with two-facedness uncomfortable. But these are precisely the kind of persons the Lord needs to be leaven in the bread and salt of the earth and light in the darkness. And this virtue is so necessary in marriage. It is hard to connect with one's spouse if one is not honest and genuine. St. Bartholomew is a powerful intercessor for those who struggle with lying, deceit, and posturing. He is a refreshing reminder of what the Lord desires in all of us: transparency, simplicity, and integrity.

Question(s) / Prayer

Lord, help us to live in the truth, since you are the Truth. Give us hearts that are sincere and transparent. Help us to be unimpressed with worldliness and moved by the virtue of genuine followers of the Gospel. Remove from us any of the duplicity that can cause would-be disciples to seek you elsewhere. Grant us the grace to speak and act with integrity and honesty—always striving to be Nathanaels in a world of superficiality and deceit.

FEAST OF THE NATIVITY OF THE BLESSED VIRGIN MARY—SEPTEMBER 8

GOSPEL: MATTHEW 1:1-16, 18-23

Meditation

Nine months after we celebrate our Lady's Immaculate Conception (December 8), we commemorate her birthday. The gospel passage taken from St. Matthew traces the Lord's genealogy from Abraham to St. Joseph. By comparison, the Gospel of St. Luke traces the Lord's genealogy from Adam onward. In the case of St. Matthew's account, he wanted to connect the Lord to his Jewish ancestry, since Matthew's intended audience was mostly Jewish. Regardless of which genealogy once reads, both Evangelists desired to make it abundantly clear that in his humanity, the Lord descended from human persons into historical circumstances. This was to demystify any suspicion that the Lord was a mythical character imagined by his followers. Although the Lord is not a human person (he is a Divine Person who assumed human nature), he nevertheless experienced the entire human experience in all things but sin. This, too, would have been a radical claim for Matthew's audience, since the Jews had no way to conceptualize the idea that God would condescend to take on humanity in order to redeem it. For them, God was so other-worldly and so foreign to their experience that the idea of God becoming man seemed audacious and absurd. By contrast, believers in the Lord assume these ideas when they think about God. But we ought not to take these realities for granted. God has truly become one like us in all things but sin and has elevated our dignity in ways unimaginable prior to his coming as man in Christ. And even as this day is dedicated to our Lady, these ideas underscore a very simply reality: everything we say or celebrate about our Lady is really a reference to the Lord.

Question(s) / Prayer

O Daughter of the Father, Mother of the Son, and Spouse of the Holy Spirit—help us to reflect the wonders God has worked in our lives by the moral standards by which we live and our willingness to proclaim the greatness of the Lord! Like you, may we learn to deflect all glory to your Son, in whom we live and move and have our being. All glory be to him, forever!

FEAST OF ST. MATTHEW, APOSTLE AND EVANGELIST—SEPTEMBER 21

GOSPEL: MATTHEW 9:9-13

Meditation

That Jesus would call a notorious sinner (in the Jewish conception) to be an Apostle and Evangelist is quite staggering, if one considers the position of tax collectors in the social strata of Judaism in antiquity. For this, the Lord was roundly criticized by the ruling religious class. The Lord makes it abundantly clear: He desires to befriend sinners in order to save them. Notice that the Lord never gets co-opted into the lives of sinners, as if he were giving tacit approval of their lifestyles. Instead, his presence purifies *them*. Jesus knows the art of engaging without giving any semblance of blessing to sin. This is a particularly important skill for all disciples of the Lord. There's a strong temptation to become isolationist (apart from the godless) on one hand, and yet another temptation to become co-opted into the lives of sinners, as if giving tacit approval of their lifestyles. Navigating through these often tricky circumstances requires prayer, the cultivation of the virtue of prudence, and the courage to set boundaries. Moreover, disciples also have to understand that they are not Jesus! They have limitations the Lord was never bound by. So this discernment requires humility and patience. Married couples are often well positioned to engage those who have not yet known the Lord, but they must do so with proper care.

Question(s) / Prayer

Thank you for befriending sinners, Lord. And help us to do the same, as our circumstances permit. Ground us in prudence and humility so that we engage sinners, even as we acknowledge our own need for conversion. Whenever we are tempted to write off the seemingly godless, grace us with the patience to engage these individuals with integrity and without moral compromise. May the strength of our marriage and our love for you inspire more couples to know you, even as we struggle daily towards holiness.

FEAST OF SS. MICHAEL, GABRIEL, AND RAPHAEL, ARCHANGELS—SEPTEMBER 29

GOSPEL: JOHN 1:47-51

Meditation

The word "angel" is taken from the Greek word that means "messenger." Archangels have delivered messages of the highest importance from God to men. The name "Michael" means "who is like God"—an allusion to his message to Lucifer when he rebelled against God and was expelled from heaven. Gabriel means "God is my strength," and Raphael means "God's remedy." Divine Revelation shows that God is actively engaged in his desire for us to become saints. He has put us in the care of these superior beings, who themselves have no physical bodies, to guide and protect us on our journey to heaven. The angels in their incorporeality remind us, too, of the importance of being attuned to the non-physical world (what we refer to in the Creed as the invisible). They remind us that beyond human sight—there is an entire world and mode of existence which we cannot fathom or truly grasp from this side of eternity. These realities should cause us to set our hearts and minds on the life of the world to come, even as we strive to perfect and sanctify our lives here on earth. The angelic world broadens our horizons to look beyond what we can observe in the physical world and strive towards very otherworldly goals.

Question(s) / Prayer

Father in heaven, it is so easy for us to lose sight of the other-worldly realities that both influence and direct our lives here and now. We can become so consumed by the many things in the material world around us that we fail to perceive forces (good and evil) working for either our salvation or our eternal ruin. Help us to cultivate a sense for the movements of grace that direct us to you. And may we always be attentive to the work of both the angels and demons in the spiritual warfare for souls.

FEAST OF ST. LUKE, EVANGELIST—OCTOBER 18
GOSPEL: LUKE 10:1-9

Meditation

At first glance, one may wonder why the Lord provided such specific instructions regarding the manner in which his disciples would conduct their ministry, acting in his name. Upon a closer look, it becomes clear that the Lord desires to form their hearts with certain dispositions as they seek out souls: First, the instruction to go penniless is intended to teach his followers not to be self-reliant, depending upon their own resources, but to trust that God will provide for all their needs. Second, the instruction to avoid greeting anyone along the way is intended to teach his followers to be focused and resolute in their mission. Third, the instruction to remain in the same house and to eat and drink whatever their hosts offer is intended to teach his followers to avoid succumbing to the temptation to go after "the better deal" or the more affluent people in a town. A disciple ought to be content with whatever Divine Providence supplies. These three virtues of dependency on God's providence, focus upon one's mission, and the humility to grow where one is planted are easily transferable into the vocation to marriage. Worldliness often breeds self-reliance, a life of distraction, and opportunism. Genuine disciples of the Lord must learn the way of the Lord, who owned nothing in this life, who was resolute in doing the Father's will, and who remained humble and meek of heart.

Question(s) / Prayer

Are we intentional in cultivating the virtues extolled in today's gospel passage? Do we allow the Lord to form us to be dependent on God's providence, focused on our sanctification, and humble enough to grow where we are planted? Or are we given to self-reliance, a life of distraction, and opportunism? Can we pivot to the life Jesus would want for us?

FEAST OF SS. SIMON AND JUDE, APOSTLES—OCTOBER 28

GOSPEL: LUKE 6:12-16

Meditation

Today's Gospel includes an important but often overlooked detail: The Lord "called his disciples to himself" (Lk 6:13). And if you look at the qualifications of those whom he called, it is evident that the Lord does not call the qualified—he qualifies those whom he calls. Their qualification is that the Lord called them to himself. They belong to him and he empowers them to act on his behalf. Similarly, married persons must rely on the Lord's qualifying them to live their vocations well. Spouses soon discover that their "resources" are quite meager compared to the challenges of living the married state well. Regardless of one's financial or social standing, grace is absolutely indispensable if a marriage is going to survive, let alone thrive. Many couples fail when they delude themselves into thinking that "their love" will sustain them throughout their lives. Couples find out soon enough that without grace, they will find enough reasons to fall out of love. The Lord calls couples to himself to sustain them and help them flourish. And just as the disciples would learn that they could do nothing without the Lord—so must married couples learn to trust that they must rely on the graces of their sacrament.

Question(s) / Prayer

Are we too reliant on our own "resources," so as to think that we will able to sustain our relationship apart from the Lord's grace? Do we realize that money cannot buy love? Do we approach our marriage with soft hearts that allow the Lord to form us and to overcome our willfulness? Do we see how the Lord called us to himself to qualify us to accomplish his mission in our lives? Do we recognize that providence brought us together and not mere chance or "fate?"

SOLEMNITY OF ALL SAINTS—NOVEMBER 1

GOSPEL: MATTHEW 5:1-12A

Meditation

There's an old saying, "Saints are not born, they're made!" With the exception of our Lady and St. John the Baptist, the saints had to pass through the crucible of internalizing and actualizing the Beatitudes, featured in today's Gospel. For the saints, observing the Ten Commandments was not enough. They strove to live the Beatitudes daily ... and succeeded by God's grace. Today's celebration commemorates all the saints whose names are known to God alone. They cooperated with grace to be transformed from sinners to saints. In our day, one of the great spiritual dangers is the presumption of one's salvation. So often at funerals, mourners comfort one another with assurances that the deceased is in "some better place" although they have no real evidence other than their own sentimentality. This presumption of salvation ignores the doctrines of hell and purgatory and makes a judgement on a person's soul, which is reserved to God alone. By contrast, the saints never presumed their salvation. In fact, the saints discovered that the closer they seemed to be getting to God, the farther away he seemed. Hence, the saints didn't think they were saints at all. It is this type of humble realism that motivated them to strive for the spiritual perfection the Gospel demands.

Question(s) / Prayer

Is sanctification a genuine personal and marital goal? Do we have the ambition to be saints? Do we invoke the intercession of the saints in our marriage? Who are our favorite saints, and why? Do we turn to them for inspiration and courage to persevere in our discipleship?

FEAST OF THE DEDICATION OF THE LATERAN BASILICA—NOVEMBER 9

GOSPEL: JOHN 2:13-22

Meditation

The Lateran Basilica is the mother church of Christendom. From the early fourth century until 1309, popes resided at the adjacent Lateran Palace. (The Vatican complex did not become the base of operations for the Church until the late fourteenth century.) Even today, the Lateran Basilica is the cathedral of the pope and his see as the Bishop of Rome. More than a celebration of the role that the Lateran complex has played in Church history, today's feast is a commemoration of the Church as an ecclesial communion. The Church is the Mystical Body of Christ and he is her head. Each member of the Church is a spiritual stone in the edifice of that communion, and together with Christ her head they constitute a living monument to the glory of the Most Holy Trinity. In today's Gospel, Jesus demonstrates his righteous indignation (not sinful anger) at those who defiled the Temple of Jerusalem, converting it to a business operation—a far cry from its intended purpose. The Gospel reminds the members of the Church that the religion founded by the Lord exists above all for the salvation of souls. In the context of marriage, the family home is a domestic church. Like the Catholic Church, it has traditions, a commitment to virtue, and rituals and meals. It is in the home that children learn about the Lord and parents renew their marital covenant in mutual love. A Catholic home is a hallowed space, and in the aggregate, Catholic homes form the larger, universal Church through the lived experience of parishes and dioceses.

Question(s) / Prayer

How connected are we to our local parish? Do we support the evangelization efforts of the pastor? Do we show our solidarity with the poor through our support of parish ministries? What is the status of our home as a domestic church? Do we see the connection between our family meals and the Mass? Is our home a place of prayer, respite, and peace? What can we do to convert our home into a genuine domestic church?

FEAST OF ST. ANDREW, APOSTLE—NOVEMBER 30

GOSPEL: MATTHEW 4:18-22

Meditation

St. Andrew can be considered a "bridge" saint in that he introduced St. Peter (his brother) to the Lord. In John's Gospel, Andrew intercedes on behalf of some Greeks visiting Jerusalem for the feast day who approach St. Philip, another apostle. Andrew connects the Greeks with the Lord (see John 12). Interestingly, one of the most ancient titles of the pope is *Pontifex Maximus* (the greatest bridge builder [between God and men and among men]). Similarly, a solid Catholic marriage can be a very effective bridge to introduce non-believers and lukewarm Catholics to the Lord. There will always be a need for Andrews in the world, especially when the zeal for souls and evangelization seems to be waning in so many parts of the world. The Church is in desperate need of witnesses to the truth of the Gospel. A holy Catholic couple can inspire those who are struggling in their marriage to cultivate virtues that are lacking. Spouses in a sacramental marriage who live their vows in fidelity and joy demonstrate that living a marriage in Christ is not only possible—it is life-giving!

Question(s) / Prayer

How do we leverage the strengths of our marriage to bring others to the Lord? Do we have the courage to witness to the centrality of a life in Christ to sustain a marriage? Can we witness in a way that is natural and not overly pietistic or inaccessible? Do we live our vows in joy in order to attract other couples to the good news of Jesus? Do we invite other couples to attend Mass with us? Would we consider hosting a Bible study?

SOLEMNITY OF THE IMMACULATE CONCEPTION OF THE BLESSED VIRGIN MARY—DECEMBER 8

GOSPEL: LUKE 1:26-38

Meditation

The dogma of the Immaculate Conception makes an audacious claim: The Church teaches that at the moment of our Lady's conception in the womb of St. Ann, she received the merits of the graces of the Passion of Jesus in an anticipatory way and was preserved from Original Sin. One may ask why she would need to be conceived without sin. The answer is simple: to pass sinless humanity on to Jesus at his conception, depicted in today's Gospel. Others may ask how Mary could receive the merits of a future event (the Passion of the Lord). Here, we have to understand that God can act outside of time since he is eternal. Even the Greeks understood different types of time: *Chronos* aligns with seconds, minutes, days, weeks, months, and years. *Kairos* describes a watershed moment, like the Immaculate Conception. The historical event took place on a particular day, and the sense of time in which God acted was also a *Kairos* moment. So God applied the graces of a future event to our Lady's soul for the sole purpose of giving her perfect humanity to pass along to Jesus. This demonstrates the breadth and depth and heights that God was willing to go to in order to save us. Our Lady's very being is a sign of God's mercy and compassion for his wayward people, in need of redemption in order to experience salvation.

Question(s) / Prayer

How would we describe our Marian devotion within our marriage? Do we truly appreciate our Lady's remarkable status as the Mother of God and our spiritual mother in the order of grace? Do we trust that she sincerely desires to aid us in our marriage, having lived that vocation herself? Do we go to our Lady with all of our intentions, asking her to perfect and refine them and to present them to the Lord? O Mary, conceived without sin, pray for us who have recourse to thee!

FEAST OF OUR LADY OF GUADALUPE—DECEMBER 12

GOSPEL: LUKE 1:26-38 OR 39-47

Meditation

There are few apparitions of our Lady that so evoke her maternal care for us. In the apparitions in Mexico in 1531, she said to St. Juan Diego, *"Listen and understand, my littlest son, let nothing frighten and afflict you or trouble your heart. ... Am I not here, I, who am your mother? Are you not under my shadow? Am I not your health? Are you not by chance held in my mantle?"* Appearing as a *mestiza* (half indigenous and half European), her vesture, posture, and gaze won over the hearts of the Aztec people and within a decade converted Latin America to Christ. Devotion to her spread all over the world, as far as the Philippines, of which she is also patroness. The image of Our Lady of Guadalupe is the only apparition where she appears pregnant. The miraculous *tilma* (poncho-like vestment) upon which she left her fabled image contains miraculous phenomena such as its own temperature (human body temperature), two heartbeats (at her heart and womb), and an alignment of stars on her mantle that match those of December 12, 1531. Our Lady's *tilma*, which hangs in the basilica in Mexico City dedicated to her, is a living image! She is a reminder that our Lady is never a passive mother, but vibrant and busy about interceding for her children.

Question(s) / Prayer

Heavenly mother, teach us to seek you with confidence—knowing that you will intercede on our behalf to the Father. May we learn to trust your solicitude for us in our every need. Teach us to ask the Father for what we truly need—those things that pertain most directly to our salvation. Whenever we feel abandoned or alone, help us to feel your maternal care and gaze. Whenever we are uncertain of our future, help us to know that you never leave our side but guide and aid us. When our faith wavers, lead us to your Son and our Savior.

FEAST OF ST. STEPHEN, PROTOMARTYR—DECEMBER 26

GOSPEL: MATTHEW 10:17-22

Meditation

Just a day after Christmas, the Church celebrates the Feast of St. Stephen, the Church's protomartyr. It is a stark reminder that the Jesus was the only person ever born to die. All other human persons were and are born to live forever. Stephen's witness would be the first among a long line of martyrs who would pay the ultimate price for the Faith in perfect imitation of Christ, who died to accomplish the Father's will. Jesus exhorts his followers to have the interior freedom not to have anxiety about their defense before persecutors—for it is the Holy Spirit that will guide and instruct them on what to say. How precious to God is the death of the martyrs! Theirs is a crown of everlasting glory!

Question(s) / Prayer

Are we prepared to die those little deaths each day—to our preferences, our opinions, our life plans, those fleeting things that we think will bring us real happiness? The martyrs remind us of what truly matters in the end: getting to heaven! Every human trapping pales in comparison. Do we have the eyes to see and embrace this simple but fundamental truth?

FEAST OF ST. JOHN, APOSTLE AND EVANGELIST—DECEMBER 27

GOSPEL: JOHN 20:1A, 2-8

Meditation

One of the distinguishing qualifications of being an Apostle was not only being chosen and called by Christ—it was also being an eyewitness to the Resurrection. The gospel passage narrates one of the major turning points in the life of St. John—Easter Sunday morning. This would be the miracle and phenomenon that would surpass all other wonders (healings, resuscitations, exorcisms) that John would witness and make a permanent and lasting impression upon him. The hope of the empty tomb leads John to faith in the Resurrection—the central mystery of Christian faith and pattern for eternal glory for all believers who are saved.

Question(s) / Prayer

Do we tend to treat the stories in the Bible as fables or myths? Do we grasp the basis for the faith of the Apostles—eyewitness testimony? Do these mysteries penetrate our souls and move us to adoration? Do we pray for deeper faith to orient our lives in a way that respects what the Lord has accomplished for us?

FEAST OF THE HOLY INNOCENTS, MARTYRS—DECEMBER 28

GOSPEL: MATTHEW 2:13-15, 19-23

Meditation

Herod's recklessness reveals that the Lord did not exempt himself, his loved ones, or innocent children from the absurdity of evil. Herod is threatened by a poor child, who does not have an army or court or political vision. The Holy Innocents are exposed to an absurd situation—guilt by association with Jesus, even if most of the parents of these children probably didn't even know the Holy Family! It requires supernatural faith to interpret this massacre as part of God's plan. A completely worldly and secular view cannot begin to make sense of its meaning. The tragedy does not require us to know the "why" behind the event—but to trust in the Lord's justice that will vindicate all injustice at the end of time.

Question(s) / Prayer

Lord, help us to trust in you, even when circumstances don't always admit of easy answers. May a supernatural outlook help us to interpret life's circumstances vis-à-vis our eternal destiny—which is already enjoyed by the Holy Innocents.

LITANY OF LIGHT

V. Lord, have mercy on us.
R. Christ, have mercy on us.
V. Lord, have mercy on us. Christ, hear us.
R. Christ, graciously hear us.
V. God the Father of Heaven, *have mercy on us.*

God the Son, Redeemer of the world, *have mercy on us.*
God the Holy Spirit, *have mercy on us.*
Holy Trinity, one God, *have mercy on us.*

Christ, Light of the World, *hear us.*
Holy Mother of God, *pray for us.*
Mother of the New Dawn, *pray for us.*

Holy Trinity, source of all light, *illuminate the darkness in our world:*
To the minds of those dimmed by sin, *bring your light.*
To the hearts of those gripped by pornography, *bring your light.*
To those suffering depression or mental illness, *bring your light.*
To the souls enslaved by substance abuse, *bring your light.*
To those burdened by same-sex attraction, *bring your light.*
To those gripped by anxiety and fear, *bring your light.*
To the hearts of those who mourn, *bring your light.*

To the souls and bodies of abusers and the abused, *bring your light.*
To those with no place to call home, *bring your light.*
To those intent on killing in the name of God, *bring your light.*
To abortion clinics, *bring your light.*
To brothels and human-trafficking locations, *bring your light.*
To hospitals, pharmacies, and nursing homes, *bring your light.*
To classrooms of despair, confusion, and falsehood, *bring your light.*
To violent and drug-infested streets, *bring your light.*
To war-torn territories, *bring your light.*
To lands darkened, flooded, or destroyed by natural disasters, *bring your light.*
Wherever there is confusion, despair, loneliness, and anger, *bring your light.*

St. Joseph, *pray for us.*
St. Mary Magdalene, *pray for us.*
St. Lucy, *pray for us.*
St. Augustine, *pray for us.*
St. Hildegard of Bingen, *pray for us.*
St. Claire, *pray for us.*
St. Albert the Great, *pray for us.*
St. Thomas Aquinas, *pray for us.*
St. Bonaventure, *pray for us.*
All the choirs of angels, *pray for us.*
Mary, Light in the Darkness, *pray for us.*

V. Light of the World, who take away the sins of the world,
R. Spare us, O Lord.
V. Light of the World, who take away the sins of the world,
R. Graciously hear us, O Lord.
V. Light of the World, who take away the sins of the world,
R. Have mercy on us.

Amen.

Composed by Carrie Gress, PhD
Imprimatur: Most Rev. Liam Cary, Bishop of Baker, OR

ABOUT THE AUTHOR

Fr. Jerome A. Magat, SThD, serves as the vice-rector, a professor of moral theology, and a seminary formator at St. Patrick's Seminary in Menlo Park, CA. Originally from Washington, DC, he was ordained for the Diocese of Arlington, VA, in 2002 and has eleven years of parish experience, in addition to twelve years of seminary formation and academic work. He has been a regular speaker on the subject of marriage, having assisted in the Diocese of Arlington's Conferences for the Engaged for nearly ten years. He holds four advanced degrees in moral theology, including two master's degrees from Mount St. Mary's Seminary in Emmitsburg, MD, and a licentiate and doctorate in moral theology from the Pontifical Lateran University (Accademia Alfonsiana) in Rome. This is his second book.

Learn more about Fr. Magat at jeromemagat.com or facebook.com/frjeromemagat and click on the QR code below to hear his homily on marriage.

Made in the USA
Columbia, SC
11 March 2025